Historic Quilts
OF THE
DAR MUSEUM

Historic Quilts
OF THE
DAR MUSEUM

• Martha Pullen's Favorite Places Series •

The Martha Pullen Company

Publisher: Martha Pullen
Editorial Direction: Kathy McMakin
Editorial Contribution: Amelia Johanson
Publications Director: Leighann Lott
Graphic Design: Courtney Kyle
Embroidery Art: Angela Pullen Atherton
Copy Editing: Karen Pyne

✦ ✦ ✦ ✦ ✦ ✦ ✦ ✦

The Martha Pullen Company
149 Old Big Cove Road
Brownsboro, Alabama 35741
www.marthapullen.com

The DAR Museum

Author and Curator of Costume and Textiles: Alden O'Brien
Museum Director and Chief Curator: Diane L. Dunkley
Curatorial Assistant: Virginia Vis
Photography: Mark Gulezian, QuickSilver Photographers
and D. James Dee (photos on pages 18, 33, 94, 96, 100, 108, and 112)

Hoffman Media, LLC.

President: Phyllis Hoffman
Vice President/Manufacturing: Greg Baugh
Digital Imaging Specialist: Clark Densmore

✦ ✦ ✦ ✦ ✦ ✦ ✦ ✦

Hoffman Media, LLC.
1900 International Park Drive, Suite 50
Birmingham, Alabama 35243

Copyright © 2011 The Martha Pullen Company, a subsidiary of Hoffman Media, LLC. All rights reserved. No part of this publication may be reproduced in any form or by any means, electronic, photocopy or otherwise without written permission from The Martha Pullen Company.

Printed in the United States of America

ISBN: 978-1-878048-63-9

CONTENTS

Early
Blue and White Crewelwork Quilt 14
Molly Lothrop's Bed Rugg 16
Wholecloth Wool Quilt 18
Glazed Wool Star Quilt 20
Copper-plate Printed Counterpane 22
Pheasant and Pomegranate Indigo Quilt 24
Martha Harness's Framed Medallion 26
Keturah Young's Crewelwork Quilt 28
Abigail Hale's Embroidered Bedspread 30

Medallion
Garnhart Eagle Quilt 32
Reverse Appliqué Flower Basket Quilt 33
Amelia's Lauck's Medallion Quilt 34
Amelia's Quilt made for William 37
Floral Roundels Medallion Quilt 38
Framed Medallion Quilt 41
Audubon Tree of Life Quilt 42
Norris Family Genealogy Quilt 44
Eliza McKee's Appliqué Vine Quilt 46

Whitework
Tree of Life Counterpane 48
Hearts and Swags Counterpane 50
French Knot Counterpane 52
Medallion and Hearts Whitework Quilt 54
Embroidered and Stuffed Whitework Quilt 56

Appliqué
Four-block Eagle Quilt 58
Louvica Houchins's Princess Feather Quilt 60
Margaret McClelland's Maze Quilt 62
Mary Sneed's Texas Baskets 64
Mary King's Appliqué Quilt 66
Ruth Jean Carter's Berries and Reel Quilt 68
Margaret McMath's Tulip Quilt 70
Garden Maze Floral Wreath Appliqué Quilt 72
Marie Webster Dogwood Quilt 74

Album
"Mary Simon" Style Baltimore Album Quilt Top 78
Andrew Jackson Commemorative Album Quilt 82
Penn Family Baltimore Album Quilt 84
Quaker Album Quilt 86
Fish Family Chintz Album Quilt 88

Pieced
Log Cabin Patchwork 92
Mrs. Francis Scott Key's Counterpane 94
Sarah Kyle's Star Quilt 96
Hanna Wallis Miller's Mosaic Quilt 98
Mildred Fox's Bethlehem Star Quilt 100
Blazing Star Wool Quilt 102
Pickle Dish Quilt 104

Crazy Quilts
Julia Hosford's Crazy Quilt 108
Anna Hall's Crazy Quilt 110
Almira Boggs's Painted Crazy Quilt 112

Embellished
Embroidered Silk Satin Bedspread 114
Victorian Crewelwork Bedspread 116
Stuffed Flower Vases Quilt 118
Embroidered Wool Counterpane 120
Elizabeth Ann's Sunburst Quilt 122
Arkansas Fritzien's Centennial Patchwork 124
Embroidered Calamanco Quilt 126

Conviction
Biblical Stories Quilt 128
Redwork Scripture Bedspread 130
Civil War Flag Bedspreads 132
Peterson's Magazine Flag Bedspread 134
Henry Clay Campaign Silk Counterpane 136
George Washington Commemorative Counterpane ... 138
Mercy Deuel's Whitework Counterpane 140

ACKNOWLEDGEMENTS

As curator of the quilt collection at the DAR Museum, I stand on some tall shoulders. Nancy Gibson, my immediate predecessor, did much during her tenure to build the collection and to publicize it through her articles in the magazine *Antiques*, The American Quilt Studies Group's scholarly journal *Uncoverings*, and elsewhere. Preceding her as curator of textiles, and also holding the position of museum director, Gloria Seaman Allen presided over not only quilts, but coverlets and samplers, adding significantly to our holdings in these collections. Her scholarship in all three areas is remarkable. Both Nancy and Gloria conducted and supervised a great deal of research on many of the quilts in the collection, notably those that were acquired during their tenures. Many of the entries in this book depend greatly on their extensive groundwork.

During my own tenure, I have been fortunate to have the guidance and help of two quilt historians who continue to give generously of their time and expertise to the DAR Museum, and guidance to me in my curatorship. Virginia Vis and Debby Cooney have conducted extensive research on our Baltimore Album quilts and many others. I continue to learn and grow as a historian through their tutelage in the nuances of quilt history. Both are crack genealogists, winkling out family histories from the slimmest of donor-provided information. Virginia has also acted as my unofficial but never unappreciated fact checker and editor. Her rigorous vigilance in restraining my stylistic sins has immeasurably improved this book.

My sincere thanks also go to the museum's registrars, Anne Ruta and Stephanie Livingston, who have patiently borne with my constant movement of both quilts and their record files—two things which tend to make registrars nervous—and assisted with collection and scanning of images. Diane Dunkley, chief curator and museum director, oversaw the book's progress and served as another pair of editorial eyes.

It has been a great pleasure and privilege to work with the Martha Pullen Company on a second book. We at the museum are indebted to Martha, herself a Distinguished Daughter, for her dedication to documenting American women's needle arts, and for her outstanding support and promotion of the DAR. Kathy McMakin, president of Martha Pullen, Inc., and Amelia Johanson, associate editor of *Sew Beautiful* magazine and the editor of this book, who have overseen the process from their end, have been a constant pleasure to work with.

Lastly we are grateful to Beverly D. West, Curator General and to Merry Ann T. Wright, President General, NSDAR, and to the Wright Administration, all of whom have provided enthusiastic support for this project.

ALDEN O'BRIEN
Curator of Costume and Textiles

THE DAR MUSEUM

Just two blocks from the White House stands a magnificent marble building in the Beaux-Arts tradition, built between 1902 and 1910 by the National Society Daughters of the American Revolution as their headquarters. Memorial Continental Hall was built to serve as offices, auditorium and a fire-proof repository for "papers and relics." It now contains one of the nation's premier genealogical libraries, surrounded by period rooms -- the core of the DAR Museum.

The National Society Daughters of the American Revolution was founded in 1890. Galvanized by being denied membership in the Sons of the American Revolution, a group of American women decided to start their own organization, honoring their ancestors who had supported the cause of liberty during the Revolutionary War. As a requirement for membership, a woman must prove her descent from someone (man or woman) who aided the American side during the war, either by fighting, feeding the troops, supplying goods or money, or serving in the new United States Government.

Since the Centennial of the Declaration of Independence in 1876, Americans had exhibited a renewed appreciation for their history, and the objects of the past. Many historical and genealogical societies were founded about this time. The DAR is one of the most successful and long-lived of those societies. From the beginning, the Daughters wanted to preserve the objects of the past, and "to study the manners and measures of those days….[and] to preserve some record of the heroic deeds of American women." From the beginning, therefore, the Daughters collected items used by their ancestors—especially handicrafts of women. Quilts, coverlets, samplers, clothing and the like found a home at the DAR long before most other museums recognized their value. Over 120 years later, the DAR Museum continues to preserve the objects and record the deeds of American women and men, exhibiting them in two galleries and 31 period rooms.

The DAR Museum quilt collection of about 300 quilts is a small but important part of the museum's holdings of over 30,000 objects. DAR members have given the majority of the collection; their family histories add historical interest and sometimes poignant stories to our knowledge of the quilts. Quilts are always on display at the DAR Museum, both on beds in the period rooms and in the museum gallery. And the entire collection can be viewed online, at the Quilt Index. You can use the searchable database at www.quiltindex.org to see any portion of our collection sorted by date, state, maker or pattern.

If planning a visit to the museum, be sure to check our opening times and exhibit schedule, as the quilts in the gallery are inaccessible during exhibit installations, and the DAR is closed on Sundays, all federal holidays, and for two weeks in the summer. For information about the DAR Museum, call 202-879-3241 or check the website at www.dar.org/museum/.

DIANE L. DUNKLEY
Museum Director and Chief Curator

CONTRIBUTORS

ALDEN O'BRIEN
Author
Curator of Costume and Textiles, DAR Museum

I came late to the history of quilts, and yet it seems a natural extension of my previous interests. Although I call myself a costume historian, I am more broadly speaking a social historian, interested especially in the lives of ordinary women. Their clothes, their quilts—their fabrics, their design, their meaning to the women who used them—it all fits. I bring to the study of quilts an eye for the decorative arts beyond textiles. I studied art history at Barnard College in New York, and have a Master's degree in Museum Studies in Costume and Textiles from the Fashion Institute of Technology.

Looking back, I think perhaps I was fated to work at the DAR. In graduate school I had an internship at a small, historic-house museum at the tip of Long Island. Once a week I would take a two-hour train ride to Oyster Bay and spend the day in an attic room at Raynham Hall Museum, cataloguing their costume and quilt collections. Raynham Hall used to be owned by the local DAR chapter; aside from being a wonderful 18th century house, it had a Revolutionary War association. Major André's treason was discovered by the daughter of the house, and from there, she sent out word that led to his capture. It seems only natural that I would end up two years later at the DAR headquarters (where a painting of André's capture hangs).

I've been at the National Society DAR since 1990, and took over the quilt collection in 2003. I love researching the women who made and owned these quilts. I love looking close-up at the exquisite, individual, sometimes quirky details of these textiles. I stand in awe of the design and needlework skills of the women whose work is represented in our collection—or any collection. I have greatly enjoyed writing the entries to this book, to bring some of our most exquisite quilts the attention they deserve and to share them with quilt lovers everywhere.

DIANE L. DUNKLEY
Museum Director and Chief Curator, DAR Museum

Diane Dunkley has been Museum Director and Chief Curator at the DAR Museum since 1990. At the headquarters of the Daughters of the American Revolution, she has coordinated several exhibits, including "Souvenirs from the Voyage of Life;" "Magnificent Intentions: Decorative Arts of the District of Columbia;" "George Washington: The Man Behind the Image;" "Bound for the West: Women and their Families on the Oregon Trail;" and "Martha Washington as an Icon of the Colonial Revival." She was co-curator of "True Love and a Happy Home: Cultural Expectations and Feminine Experiences in Victorian America," and "Talking Radicalism in a Greenhouse: Women Writers and Women's Rights." She was the lead curator of the ground-breaking exhibition "Forgotten Patriots: African American and American Indian Service in the American Revolution." Her recent exhibition projects include a major loan exhibition celebrating 250 years of Wedgwood.

Prior to coming to the DAR, Ms. Dunkley was with the Colonial Williamsburg Foundation for 10 years, serving as Manager of the Governor's Palace and as Curator of Carter's Grove, a James River plantation house. She has written articles about Carter's Grove and the Colonial Revival for *Colonial Williamsburg*, and for *The Interpreter*, both publications of the Colonial Williamsburg Foundation.

She is a graduate of East Carolina University, and holds a master's degree in history from the College of William and Mary. As a student at William and Mary, she worked in costume as a historic interpreter at Colonial Williamsburg. Although as a senior in high school she was a Betty Crocker Homemaker of Tomorrow, she reluctantly admits that she no longer is able to find time to practice the art of the needle.

MARK GULEZIAN
Photographer

Mark Gulezian began QuickSilver Photographers in 1981 in Washington, D.C. to provide professional-quality photography to artists, museums and institutions. His photography of artwork and museum objects has appeared in books and other publications worldwide.

VIRGINIA VIS
Curatorial Assistant, DAR Museum

After fourteen years as Wardrobe Supervisor for the Arena Stage in Washington, D.C., Virginia Vis began her own business cleaning and repairing quilts and other textiles in 1994. In addition to being Project Manager for the Quilt Index at the DAR Museum in 2006, she has been a volunteer in the museum's quilt collection since 2002. While working with Curator Alden O'Brien, she compiled the Museum's educational slide program titled "Masterpieces of the DAR Quilt Collection" and assisted with the "Quilts of a Young Country" loan exhibit at The International Quilt Festival in Houston, Texas in the fall of 2008.

DAR MUSEUM

INTRODUCTION

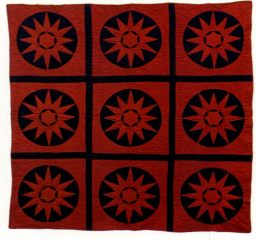

The quilt collection at the DAR Museum is known worldwide as a premier collection of early American quilts. It is actually a rather small one, with a few more than 300 quilts. But they are wonderful examples of early American quilt history. More than half of our quilts were made before 1850, and for more than two-thirds we can provide known makers or at least provenance from a certain family. We generally do not collect 20th century quilts, but we have a few examples of the quilting revival of the 1920s and '30s.

The quilts are just one part of our textile holdings. We also have more than 300 samplers and schoolgirl needleworks, more than 220 woven coverlets, a costume collection, and scores of hand-woven household linens. In addition, what we loosely call the "quilt collection" comprises unfinished quilt tops, unquilted and embroidered counterpanes, Marseilles and Bolton-type woven bedspreads, and even a few knitted and crocheted bedcovers. All these textiles are part of a collection of American decorative arts comprising more than 30,000 pieces of furniture, silver and base metals, ceramics and glass, paintings and more.

For this book, we have selected about sixty of our most aesthetically appealing and historically interesting quilts and counterpanes. Each entry describes the quilt and provides a summary of what we know of its maker and history. Being the museum of the Daughters of the American Revolution, and therefore rather interested in genealogy—and having one of the world's best genealogy libraries downstairs from our offices—we tend to dig deeply into each quilt's family history. Thus, this book may contain more detail than is found in many quilt books. Preparing this book spurred us to look more closely at the information we already have. In some cases, we had to toss what we thought we knew completely out the window. In other cases, we verified donor information and found extra details. In several instances, the donor's information was a useful starting-point, but some details were confused. This project has given us the opportunity to correct and improve upon what we knew about many of the quilts, which enhances our understanding of their history.

Our sections are presented in loosely chronological order. We have also created two thematic sections, "Embellishments" and "Convictions." Embellishments includes quilts that stand out especially because of

DAR MUSEUM

the extent and quality of techniques used beyond piecing, appliqué and quilting, namely embroidery or stuffed work. Naturally, other sections include splendid examples of embroidery and stuffed work as well, but we chose to highlight some examples in the Embellishments section.

Similarly, the Convictions section contains examples of pieced, appliqué and embroidered quilts and counterpanes. They are notable, however, for expressing religious, political or personal statements. In the 19th century, it was considered unladylike and entirely inappropriate for women to speak publicly or involve themselves in the issues of their day. Of course, some women did involve themselves in charitable and faith-based organizations, which touched on social issues of their day, and some worked in more political movements such as abolition and temperance. During the Civil War, women on both sides were enormously active in support of their causes, and in the last quarter of the century, increasing numbers of women felt it their duty to embrace more political topics such as food safety and child labor.

But for much of the time, women's voices were muffled by convention. For some, the products of their needle could express in the appropriate domestic sphere what they could not proclaim elsewhere. Here, then, are some textiles from our collection, which express opinions, loyalties or simply, in, for example, Mercy Deuel's case, proclaim a sense of self. In a wider sense, each product of a woman's needle is an expression of self in some way; choosing her fabrics and colors, patterns or blocks and their arrangements, she proclaims her skill, taste and ability to create something beautiful. This book is a celebration of these products of early American women's needles, preserved and honored at the DAR Museum.

Blue and White
CREWELWORK QUILT

About 1780

"The spring looms recently introduced into the manufacturing town of Prosperous were not, always as first reported, for the purposes of the broadcloth manufacture, but for the purposes of weaving and elegant counterpanes, the warp and weft of which are to be of the best and finest cotton yarn, and which have of late been brought to the greatest perfection in this kingdom."

—"PHILADELPHIA," *The New-Haven Gazette*, April 3, 1788

This Puritan star block pattern quilt of about 1840 is backed with a much earlier crewel-embroidered linen panel, which originally would have been part of a matched set of bed hangings. A sole surviving valance, donated at the same time as the quilt, uses coordinating blue crewelwork motifs. The crewel-embroidered panel on the back of this quilt would have been either the unquilted "counterpane" on top of the bed, or the "head cloth," the piece that hung on the wall behind the bed. These bed linens were part of Tryphena Montague's trousseau or wedding linens when she married Caleb Hubbard in 1780. Tryphena died in 1788, and her husband remarried. It is curious that the counterpane apparently did not descend through any of Tryphena's children, but instead was donated by a descendant of Tryphena's brother. Five shades of blue are used to create stylized floral sprays typical of colonial-era crewelwork. Chain stitch and closed herringbone stitch are used for the stems and outlines, orderly rows of seed stitch for the decorative petals, and mostly long-and-short stitch and Roumanian couching stitches for the solid areas. Pencil lines outlining the design are visible in the spots where the wool has been lost. The quilting was done for the Puritan star quilt in which pieced blocks alternate with plain blocks. The pieced stars are outline quilted, and the plain blocks are quilted with a hanging diamond grid.

Like so many crewelwork-embroidered bed linens, this piece was preserved by reusing it to make a new object, in this case, the back of a pieced quilt made by a later generation. Whether this was pure New England frugality, or whether the vintage handwork gave its owner pleasure hidden under the newer quilt, we cannot know, but we can appreciate its having been saved for us to enjoy.

85 in. wide by 93 in. long
Made by Tryphena Montague Hubbard (1757-1788)
Sunderland, Massachusetts
2001 Gift of Fanny Montague Stockbridge

"The intention of your being taught needlework, knitting, and such like, is not on account of the intrinsic value of all you can do with your hands, which is trifling, but to enable you to judge more perfectly of that kind of work, and to direct the execution in others."

"A FATHER'S ADVICE TO HIS DAUGHTERS," *The Christian's Scholar's and Farmer's Magazine*, August/September 1789

Molly Lothrop's Bed Rugg

About 1780-1810

The "bed rugg" (now more commonly spelled with one "g") was defined in a 1730 English dictionary as a "shaggy coverlet for the bed." The name "rug" seems apt, as its shag pile appears more suited to the floor than a bed. This one is shaggy indeed; its thick multi-ply wool thread is embroidered in running stitch on a coarse brown wool ground, and then cut to create a heavy pile resembling a carpet when the wool threads unravel slightly. This distinctive technique was popular during the 18th century in New England, where a cold climate and un-insulated houses would have made such a heavy bed covering welcome. Warm body heat would have been trapped between the fibers, just as it is between wool or down stuffing of other types of bed coverings.

This particular design is unique to New London County in southern Connecticut. The New London bed rugs feature enormous carnations and roses, rising in twining stems with enormous leafy fronds, surrounded by a border of equally large carnations in meandering vines. The stems often rise from a large squat vase or decorative pot.

Of the over fifty surviving New England bed rugs, many have dates in their design, ranging from 1722 to 1819. As we do not have a date on this example, we must use the date range of similar rugs from New London County to guess at when it was made. The Connecticut bed rugs are often executed in shades of tan and brown similar to Molly Lothrop's bed rug here, but may also be made in shades of blue and occasionally other colors; some use flat embroidery rather than shag. More than a dozen similar rugs exist with family connections to the same few towns. Genealogical research reveals that many of the makers of the New London County bed rugs are related—not surprisingly for early New England small towns, but possibly helping to explain the similarity in design.

The DAR's example was cut down at some point on the right side and at the bottom, and possibly a little at the top. Originally, the bordering flower vine would have been intact along the sides and bottom.

This rug's maker's name, Molly Lothrop, is embroidered near the top edge. But there are three candidates for this identity. Mary "Molly" Stark of Lebanon, Connecticut married her cousin James Lothrop in 1780, and she may have made the rug after her marriage. However, Molly's aunt, who was also her mother-in-law, was also named Mary (Stark) Lothrop. If she were also called Molly, it could be her bed rug instead. The fact that James Lothrop had a sister Mary, who never married and therefore would always have been named Lothrop—possibly called Molly—further muddies the waters. All we can now be certain of is that this bed rug belongs not to New Hampshire, as the family believed, but to New London County, Connecticut, with its stylistic cousins.

83.5 in. wide by 73 in. long
Made by Molly Lothrop
New London County, Connecticut
1173 Gift of Mrs. Belle Case

Wholecloth Wool Quilt

About 1790

Wholecloth quilts, made of one fabric sewn in edge-to-edge strips, were more common than pieced ones in early America. Wool ones, with wool tops and backed and filled with wool, were popular in New England and seldom seen further south. This fabric has often been called "linsey-woolsey," but in fact, it is not a linen-wool blend, but entirely wool. Its slight sheen identifies it as calamanco, or "glazed" wool. "Glazed" is a misnomer, as it implies a substance was applied to the wool to give it a sheen. The sheen was achieved by rolling heavy metal cylinders over the woven cloth, pressing down so that the microscopic "scales" of the wool fibers were flattened and aligned, allowing light to bounce off them. The sheen would have given a little extra light and detail in an otherwise dark room. The solid color wool shows to advantage the elaborate, large-scale floral and foliate quilted designs. This example sets off its stylized flowers and feather fronds with a background of closely set parallel lines on the diagonal, which make the designs stand out in contrast. The lower corners have been cut out to accommodate the posts of the bed, a treatment fairly common in New England.

The precise maker of this quilt is unknown. Donor history attributed it to Mary Chase Stevens of Unity, in southern Maine, but recent research has revealed that Mary was born long after this quilt was made (and before Unity became a town). Presumably a maternal forbear of Mary's made it, but we cannot know which relation deserves the credit. Whoever the maker, an all-wool quilt such as this would have been appreciated in the winters of Maine.

87 in. wide by 100 in. long
Made by a member of the Chase or Stevens family
Unity, Maine
8 stitches per inch
3590   Gift of Mrs. Wesley W. Blair

"She has twenty feather-beds more than she can use, and lately another sale has supplied her with a proportionable number of blankets, a large roll of linens for sheets, and five quilts for every bed, which she bought because the feller told her that, if she would clear his hands, he would let her have a bargain."

—"ACCOUNT OF A BUYER OF BARGAINS," *The American Museum*, April 1787

DAR MUSEUM

*"The bed linen, though coarse is beautifully white, and the patchwork quilt
was made by Mary at hours borrowed from sleep."*

—"BENEVOLENCE," *The Youth's Companion,* April 19, 1839

Glazed Wool Star Quilt

About 1775-1800

Preparing this book has led us to delve into family histories for many quilts which we've had for decades. The name of this quilt's maker has been a mystery since it was donated 100 years ago. We began to piece together clues based on the cross-stitched initials, H, J and S on the back, which almost certainly are contemporary to the quilt. The initials are arranged to indicate a couple with names beginning with H and J, sharing a surname beginning with S. No such surname can be found in the donor's family tree. She inherited the quilt from a great-uncle, Silvester Jacobs; but could it perhaps have come from his wife Cynthia's side of the family? Luckily, we also own Cynthia's daughter's family record needlework, which tells us Cynthia's maiden name was Stearns. Eureka! We cannot find a couple with initials H and J among her siblings, parents or grandparents, so we still cannot pin down a maker within the likely timeframe of the quilt's making. However, we can surmise that it came from some branch of Cynthia's family in Worcester County, Massachusetts.

The center medallion is a 49-inch-square pieced eight-pointed star. The design marks a transition from the more common wholecloth quilts of the 18th century, towards more common use of piecing and the framed medallion layout. Piecing and appliqué designs were used more often after 1800. The blue and green wools are approximately half-inch woven stripes, alternating a satin weave with a 2/1 (over two threads, under one) twill. Both these are highly "glazed," that is, the fabric has been pressed to give the wool the characteristic sheen of calamanco. The quiltmaker has taken trouble to align the stripes where the blue and green pieces meet; often, a satin stripe will line up with a satin stripe, other times a twill will meet a satin; but the edges of the stripes are at least always aligned.

The red wool is a plain weave, and the backing is an unbleached, natural off-white plain-weave wool. The quilting is an on-point grid. Overall, it is a relatively simple design, thoughtfully executed by a skilled needlewoman, resulting in a bold visual impact.

82.5 in. wide by 86.5 in. long
Probably made by a member of the Stearns family
Probably made in Worcester County, Massachusetts
8 stitches per inch
6521   Gift of Floretta Vining

"John Burger, returns his thanks, to his friends and former customers, and takes this method to inform them that he has removed from Barclay-Street to Maiden Lane, the corner of Green-Street, a few doors below The Oswego Market, where he carries on the business of COPPER-PLATE PRINTING in all various branches."

Copper-plate Printed Counterpane

About 1790-1800

Charming scenes of plump children at play decorate this simple bedspread. Wholecloth quilts and single-layer counterpanes were common alternatives to quilts as bed coverings. The modern term "summer spread" suggests that these were only seasonal choices, but many beds were covered year-round with simple counterpanes such as these. This one is made of seven pieces: four vertical lengths with three additional short pieces above them. It is bound with a plain white cotton tape on all four sides.

Copper-plate printing used the same technique and materials on cotton as engravings on paper. The copper engravings permitted extremely fine lines with delicate details not achievable in woodblock prints, the more usual format for textile printing. This particular design is English, featuring engravings by Francesco Bartolozzi, the official engraver to King George III and co-founder of the Royal Academy in London. The designs were based on a series of watercolors and drawings by the English artist William Hamilton. As Hamilton's scenes were engraved by Bartolozzi in 1787-88, they cannot have appeared on fabric much before 1790.

Scenes of sports and games were quite popular both in engravings and adapted for textiles throughout the 18th century, but these children playing were even more widely enjoyed. Martha Washington made an unfinished spread, now at Mount Vernon, using corner pieces made from the same fabric as the DAR Museum's. At least six other copper-plate-printed cottons were made using scenes most likely taken from Hamilton's series, and they were even printed on china. Such widespread use of these images of children reflects the late-18th century's idealization of childhood.

In the DAR's counterpane, six scenes depict children feeding poultry and playing various games including marbles and "London Bridge." The scenes are bordered by vines with leaves and pods. Although greatly faded in many of the pieces, the charm of the scenes, when viewed up close, is undiminished.

89 in. wide by 90 in. long
Unknown Maker
Probably Made in United States
52.59   Gift of Caroline How Collier Russell

"I have subjoined the common way to dye woolen blue in Europe. Indigo, Pot or Pearl-Ash will dissolve in water. Dissolve the Pot or Pearl-Ash with a gentle heat, a shining copper-coloured skin will soon cover the surface; when stirred, a large blue froth will rise, and the liquid below will appear a deep green. Woollen, yarn or cloth, wants no other preparation than moistening with warm water; then dip it in this hot liquor, it comes out a good green, and will almost instantly change into a fine blue by being exposed to air."

"LETTER TO THE EDITOR FROM BERNARD ROMANS," The Royal American Magazine, January 1774

Pheasant and Pomegranate Indigo Quilt

About 1750-75

Wholecloth quilts were by far the most common type of quilt in early America, contrary to earlier myths that our colonial forebears pieced scraps together out of frugality. This is the earliest quilt in the DAR Museum's collection, and it represents the bold aesthetic of early to mid-18th century design. Blue and white indigo patterns were popular in colonial America during this period, but a good deal of mystery surrounds the origin of these prints. Some scholars have suggested that at least some of them may have been printed in the North American colonies, but it seems highly questionable that colonial American dyers and printers had the artistic and technical expertise to carry out the designs. A surviving English textile pattern book of the period contains numerous indigo designs, including several that can be matched with extant American quilts, so clearly many were being made in Europe. These indigos do not appear in European collections, but perhaps they were made exclusively for the colonial export market. Unless new, reliably documented examples turn up, the question of their origins will remain unsettled.

Large-scale, bold designs are the most common style in these blue and white designs. Large exotic birds such as peacocks, parrots and pheasants with Indian or vaguely Eastern-inspired flowers and leaves were common motifs. This pheasant-and-pomegranate print is found in several other quilts and textile fragments in American museum collections, including the Shelburne and Metropolitan Museums and Winterthur.

Although colonial quilt makers were not piecing scraps, they were still frugal with their cloth, which was expensive at the time. The top is composed of six pieces joined without any attempt to match the pattern at the seams. Too much costly fabric would be wasted in that effort, especially with such a large-scale design. The backing is five pieces of plain white cotton. The quilt is scantly filled with cotton batting, and quilted in the center in a simple 1-inch grid design on point. There are two quilted borders: an inner one 10 inches wide, in a geometric design; and an 11-inch outer border of overlapping arches filled in with alternating grid and arch designs. Like several other indigo quilts of its time, it is bordered with a simple indigo border design 1-1/4 inches wide; it is finished with a knife edge and backed with plain cotton.

The quilt is said to have been made by a member of the Vedder family of Schenectady, New York, but as the Vedders were numerous, there is no way to pin down a single maker or even a probable branch of the family. Many of the surviving indigo quilts, bed hangings and fragments have New York origins, from Long Island to the Hudson River Valley, often with a Dutch provenance like the Vedder family's.

85 in. wide by 93 in. long
Made by a member of the Vedder Family in or near Schenectady, New York
5-6 stitches per inch
2000.12   Friends of the Museum Purchase

DAR MUSEUM

"By this time our mistress arrived at home; where the first thing she did was to dispose of us in a richly embroidered Needle-case, which, along with a new thimble and scissors, was deposited in a fine work-bag."

—"THE ADVENTURES OF NEEDLE," *The Atheneum or, Spirit of the English Magazines*, February 1, 1823

DAR MUSEUM

Martha Harness's
FRAMED MEDALLION

About 1794-1817

Family history tells us that a very young Martha Harness made the center medallion of this quilt beginning at the age of about six, assisted by her mother, Elizabeth Yoakum Harness, and that Martha continued to work her way to the outer borders. This story is supported by the fact that the outermost border with its simple leafy vine on three sides (the fourth side being only white stuffed work) is made of a blue cotton print not found in the inner areas of the quilt. The center and first two borders share the same assortment of blue and pink prints. Even the cotton ground and backings differ, the outer border not matching the rest of the quilt. The entire outer border thus appears to have been sewn to the rest of the quilt at a later date. Martha may have returned to her childhood needlework shortly before her marriage, to make the quilt large enough for a bed.

The center medallion on point, with its sawtooth border and concentric borders of floral and grape vines, is a style typical of quilts in Maryland and Virginia at the turn of the 19th century. The first border's tulip baskets in each corner recall Pennsylvania Dutch tulips, echoing Martha's parents' German heritage (her grandparents, born in Germany, emigrated from Pennsylvania to Virginia in the 1730s). In the second border, four grape clusters in a sort of pinwheel arrangement (also reminiscent of Pennsylvania Dutch motifs) at each corner cleverly solve the quilter's constant dilemma of how to turn a corner. The grapes are given a slight three-dimensionality, having been made of circles larger than each grape and loosely folded under before being stitched to the ground fabric. Embroidery thread embellishes the vine, to give the tendrils characteristics of grapevines. Between the appliqué flowers and vines, handsome stuffed-work medallions, flowers, leaves and (in the outermost border) feather fronds further embellish this handsome quilt. The remainder of the quilting is echo and stipple quilting. The restrained color palette—white with three blue and white prints and a few light pink flowers—is not only pleasing, but is perfectly balanced by the elaborate stuffed work.

117 in. wide by 108 in. long
Made by Martha Harness (1788-1854), assisted by Elizabeth Yoakum Harness (1743?-1815)
Moorefield, Hardy County, Virginia (now West Virginia)
8-11 stitches per inch
2005.38   Gift of Connie Wulfman

Early Quilts

"Quiltings appear to be two distinct cloths, tied, as it were, together,
by stitches which go through both cloths,
and in some cases, as in bed-quilts there is a third shuttle, which throws in a quantity
of coarsely spun cotton, to serve as a kind of wadding."

"ACCOUNT OF THE ENGLISH COTTON MANUFACTORY,"
The Literary Magazine and American Register, October 1805

Keturah Young's Crewelwork Quilt

1806

Keturah Young, daughter of a Revolutionary war soldier from Long Island, finished this quilt and dated it March, 1806, at the age of eighteen. Perhaps she, like many girls of her generation, made it in general anticipation of marriage; however, she never did marry, and died at the age of eight-two in 1860.

Within these basic facts lies a rather sad tale: at the time of her father's death in 1816, he was one of the town poor, along with his daughter. Keturah spent most of the rest of her life either living in the town's poorhouse, or being "hired out" to live and work in other houses in her neighborhood. From at least 1827 to 1831, she was hired out to the home of her brother, Enoch. Was this a comfort or a humiliation? We cannot know. It helps explain, however, how the quilt came to be passed down: the donor was a descendant of Enoch and his wife Polly. Did Keturah leave it behind as partial payment for her room and board? Or was she able to keep it until her death, and it only then reverted to her brother?

Twenty-two crewel-embroidered motifs have been appliquéd onto an off-white linen ground. They were reused from 18th century bed linens—whether a bed covering or bed curtains or other parts of the bed furnishings, we can't be sure. A block-printed cotton border, probably English and dating to about the 1770s or 1780s, forms the border. The quilt is backed with coarser cotton. The crewelwork appliqués are unquilted, while the background around them, both in the center field and the corners, is quilted in a scallop or clamshell pattern; the printed cotton borders are quilted in chevrons. Keturah cross-stitched her name and "March 1806" between the crewel sprigs along the left side. Her initials "K" and "Y" are executed in rows of openwork eyelets, which subtly set them apart from the rest of each word.

The extent to which quilts were made from "scraps" has been vastly exaggerated in quilt literature, and historians now try to rectify the record by stressing that most quilts were made from purpose-bought fabrics. Crewelwork, however, seems to have been recycled often, the linen ground having deteriorated while the colorful and beautiful embroidery survived to be treasured in a new incarnation. Knowing that Keturah was living in poverty at least by 1816 gives us further insight into the making of the quilt: reused bed hangings and a twenty-year-old printed cotton were probably the best textiles she had at hand when she made her quilt in 1806. Striving for fashion and beauty, she made an exquisite quilt, and unlike many of her fellow quilt makers, she truly did need to reuse old fabrics. We are fortunate that decades of economic hardship and lack of her own home did not prevent the preservation of this handsome quilt.

Made by Keturah Young (1788-1860)
Aquebogue, Long Island, New York
6-7 stitches per inch
64.133 Gift of Marjorie Young Tyte in memory of her mother, Helen Hallock Young

Abigail Hale's EMBROIDERED BEDSPREAD

About 1778

The center of this counterpane is made of two strips of linen, with additional strips forming a flounce to hang down the sides of the bed, edged with a 6-inch hand-knotted fringe; gathering at the corners at the foot of the bed would have made the flounces hang neatly. The flounce is embroidered similarly to the top of the bed, although some of its embroidery is now lost, and much of it has lost its color. In fact, the flounces' color-loss suggests that the entire spread may originally have been a much deeper blue, which would have given it a more striking appearance.

The motifs throughout are stylized, exotic floral vines and a small "Tree of Life" floral spray in the center. Although embroidered in only one color and in silk thread, they resemble crewelwork. Tudor (flat-petalled) roses, carnations and pomegranates alternate with seemingly imaginary flora, the overall style influenced both by Indian textiles and Jacobean embroidery. Featherstitch is used throughout, with herringbone stitch filling some of the leaves and flowers, and cross-stitching on others. The same flowers appear on the flounce in a lighter blue, but are less well-executed.

Abigail Page married Moses Hale in 1778, and may have made this before her marriage in Haverhill, Massachusetts (they later moved to New Hampshire). Her name is embroidered in cross-stitched letters beneath the center motif. A date of 1776 has been embroidered underneath Abigail's name, but in backstitch and in brown, almost certainly added after the original embroidery and therefore somewhat suspect. Later family members often wishfully ascribe family heirlooms to famous dates. However, girls did sew household linens in the years leading up to their marriages, even before they knew whom they would marry; so it is not impossible that this might have been started in 1776. It could equally have been made in the years following Abigail's marriage. Whatever the case, Abigail created an elegant spread, and we are fortunate that it survives.

74 in. wide by 78 in. long (including 6 in. fringe)
Made by Abigail Page Hale (1755-1834)
Haverhill, Massachusetts
***61.89** Gift of Maybelle Still*

"Cut a point of mottled soap into thin slices; put it into a pan with a quarter of an ounce of potash, and one ounce of pearl-ash; then pour a pail of boiling water on it: let it stand till it is quite dissolved; then pour hot and cold water into your scouring tub, with a bowl of your solution of soap. Put in your counterpane, and beat it well out with a doll, often turning the counterpane over in the tub."

"For Scouring Thick Cotton; as Counterpanes, Quilts, etc.," *Godey's Lady's Book*, March 1832

91 in. wide by 91.5 in. long
Made by Anna Catherine Hummel Markey Garnhart
(1773-1860)
Made for and quilted by Anna Catherine Markey
(1824-1907)

DAR MUSEUM

Garnhart Eagle Quilt

Made about 1825; Quilted in 1846

Anna Catharine Garnhart, about 1850

Remarkably, at least twelve quilts attributable to Anna Catherine Garnhart survive, three in museums (two at the DAR) and the rest still owned by descendants of the quiltmaker. Anna Catherine, née Hummel, first married David Markey and had two sons and eventually eleven grandchildren. She is known to have made a quilt for each grandchild, and we know the recipient of all but two of the surviving quilts. Each quilt can be dated approximately based on its fabrics and overall style, and taking into account the birth date of the grandchild who received it. But since so many similar quilts were produced together, exact dates are elusive. It is possible that some were made far in advance of the birth of the eventual recipient.

Seven full-size quilts, four with eagles at the center and three with baskets, and four crib-size quilts survive with certain connections to Anna Catherine (who married Henry Garnhart after being widowed). Another quilt attributed to her is in a Mariner's Compass design. Thus, more quilts survive than there were grandchildren. But each of the crib quilts descended in the same branch as a larger quilt, and there are three children for whom we have no quilt. As a result, not every grandchild can be matched to a quilt.

Anna Catherine repeated a certain recognizable format, with variations from quilt to quilt. She put large urns or baskets of flowers, sometimes in conjunction with eagles in the style of the Seal of the United States, in a large central medallion. This is always bordered by some sort of reverse appliqué leafy vine. Outside of the vine, more floral arrangements of various sizes are arranged, with a sawtooth border and sometimes a final outer border of printed cotton. Here, the flower baskets and urns in the outer border are interspersed on the sides with four bright green fern fronds, and the border is surrounded by a small sawtooth border. The outermost border is a larger, pointier sawtooth.

Appliqué and reverse appliqué are both used. The floral baskets and urns are appliqué. The eagle and stars, leafy vine around the center medallion, bright green ferns, and outermost sawtooth border are reverse appliqué. The extensive use of reverse appliqué is one of Garnhart's quilts' signature characteristics.

The grandchild for whom the quilt was made, Anna Catherine Markey, recorded that she herself did the quilting on her grandmother's gift, in 1846 prior to her marriage. The field is quilted in diamonds, outline, feather, grid, with sunflowers in the four corners. The three borders are quilted in a continuous running feather and a chevron pattern.

< Reverse Appliqué Flower Basket Quilt
About 1825-40
93 in. wide by 95 in. long
Made by Anna Catherine Hummel Markey Garnhart (1773-1860)
Made for John Hanshaw Markey (1835-1899) Frederick, Maryland
7-8 stitches per inch
91.463   Gift of Mr. and Mrs. Willard Markey

Amelia Lauck's MEDALLION QUILT

1823

Amelia Heiskell Lauck and her husband Peter Lauck were children of German immigrants who moved from Pennsylvania to Winchester, Virginia in the mid-18th century. Peter fought in the American Revolution, was captured at the Battle of Quebec, and lost hearing in one ear from proximity to cannon fire. He returned to Winchester to abandon his trade as a potter and become proprietor of the Red Lion Tavern. Amelia gave birth to eleven children, six of whom lived to adulthood.

Amelia made at least four similar quilts, each a masterpiece of American folk art. Three of the quilts are inscribed to three of these children, while the fourth, lacking an inscription, was probably made for another. It seems likely that she made at least two more quilts for the remaining children, which appear to be lost. Two of the surviving quilts are in the DAR Museum's collection and the other two are owned by Colonial Williamsburg. Virginia quilts from before the Civil War are rather rare, but the fact that four quilts survive by one maker, all dating to the mid-1820s, and each of such superior design and execution, is unheard of.

Amelia Heiskell Lauck painted by Jacob Frymire in 1801
Collection of the Museum of Early Southern Decorative Arts, Old Salem Museums & Gardens

Amelia's quilts are remarkably similar in design. She was fond of the framed medallion layout, the most common quilt design of the first quarter of the 19th century. All four quilts use the same printed floral cotton flowers and stems in the centers, and three use the same bird print. All use pink or pinkish-red printed cottons pieced in "Delectable Mountain" borders, with eight-pointed stars at the corners. These alternate with plain white borders adorned with stuffed-work. Delectable Mountain borders, and the similar but simpler Sawtooth border, were popular in Virginia and Maryland quilts of this time.

In the DAR's quilt made for Amelia's only daughter Rebecca, printed lily-like flowers and stems have been cut and arranged into a wreath in the center medallion, with birds at each corner and another at the top of the wreath. A cluster of lilies is placed inside the

> "The day is set the ladies met, And at the frame are seated;
> In order placed they work in haste, To get the quilt completed,
> While fingers fly their tongues they ply, And animate their labours,
> By counting beaux, discussing clothes, Or talking of their neighbors."
>
> –Excerpt from "THE QUILTING," a poem in *Boston Masonic Mirror*, July 24, 1823

wreath at the center. A quilted and stuffed eagle in the center medallion carries a banner in its beak with the initials "R.C" and "I.C." (the letters I and J being used interchangeably at that time). A backstitched inscription in the outermost border reads "Made by Amelia Lauck in the 62 year of her Age April 15 1823."

The four quilts share almost identical motifs in the borders. Amelia excelled in stuffed-work, both in the white spaces created between the pieced areas in the Delectable Mountains borders and in the all-white borders. The center medallions of the two DAR quilts are alone in featuring stuffed-work American eagles holding arrows in their talons and banners in their beaks, with inscriptions identifying the recipient of each quilt being stitched in the banners. In the first pieced borders of all four quilts, we find an infinite variety of stuffed flowers including daisies, tulips and pinks, none an exact repeat of the others. The two quilts with outer "mountain" borders have alternating feather fronds and grape clusters.

While making a quilt at the age of sixty-two—or making two, for one of Williamsburg's quilts is dated the same year—is worthy of admiration, it is almost certain that Amelia had help, probably including help from her husband's enslaved African-American servants. Quilting was always, to a greater or lesser extent, a cooperative activity among women, and Southern women would have made use of skilled seamstresses in their household. The 1820 census shows five female slaves in the Lauck household. While they were undoubtedly needed to wait on customers at the Red Lion Tavern, they probably helped the Laucks in their household as well. Amelia certainly would have designed the quilts and the quilting patterns, but relied on help for sewing, to what extent we cannot know.

Amelia's Quilt made for William
About 1823

Amelia gave this nearly identical quilt to her son William and his wife Eliza Sowers, who married in 1830. Originally, it also had an outer Delectable Mountains border, which was cut off at some point after it appeared intact in a 1920s photo. The medallion's wreath and corner birds are from the same fabrics as those found in the other three quilts by Amelia. Like Rebecca's, William's quilt has an American eagle quilted inside the wreath, with a banner in his beak proclaiming that the quilt was "Presented by their Mother to W&E L." The quilt passed down through William's descendants until its donation to the DAR Museum.

85 in. wide by 87 in. long
Made by Amelia Lauck
Winchester, Virginia
9-11 stitches per inch
2006.3.1   Gift of Sally Lauck Harris

Floral Roundels
MEDALLION QUILT

Made about 1815-1825; Quilted about 1870

Although we do not know the specific maker of this quilt, we know it originated in South Carolina, where chintz appliqués floating on a white field were a popular variation on the medallion format. Here, a large central roundel with an overflowing fruit basket is surrounded by smaller floral roundels and other shapes. The triangular pieces immediately above, below and to each side of the central circle were cut from the corners outside the circle. The long sides of the triangles are noticeably curved, showing where they adjoined the large circle. Alternating with the curved triangles to form a sort of border around the center medallion are sixteen-pointed star or wreath-like shapes, with eight-pointed star cutouts. These are cut from floral chintz with a blue honeycomb or net-like background. This fabric is repeated in the eight-pointed stars in the corners of the quilt. A third fabric appears in the ten smaller roundels or medallions, which form the second "border" around the center medallion. Finally, a fourth fabric forms the outer border and edge of the quilt. It is pieced in four strips, with the top and bottom edges extending the width of the quilt, and the sides fitting inside those borders.

The center medallion is English block-printed cotton of about 1815. English printed cottons had of course been imported into America since colonial times, and the English textile industry was still, at this time, more advanced than our own. Large pre-printed panels intended for use in quilts and seat covers were popular from the late 18th through the early 19th centuries.

The panel here, too large for chair seats, appears to have been made for use in quilts; and since at least six other quilts using the same central design are preserved in museum collections, it was clearly quite popular. Most of the quilts featuring this particular fabric were made near port cities such as Philadelphia, Baltimore and Charleston—where English fabrics were readily available, and where plenty of fashionable

> *"The more she thought it over, the more certain she could well spare the package of old-fashioned quilts which had fallen to her share when her Aunt Deborah's goods were portioned out."*
> —"THE EXTRA BLANKET," by J.E. MCC, *Arthur's Illustrated Home Magazine*, March 1875

customers were eager to buy the latest off the ships. The DAR Museum owns a quilt with the same center panel (shown on the next page), in an entirely different style of quilt, equally typical of South Carolina, where it too was made. This second quilt keeps the square panel intact and surrounds it with a series of concentric floral printed borders.

The entire quilt has been quilted in a fan pattern. This style of quilting did not originate until several generations after the quilt was made, and dates to about 1870, presumably carried out by a later generation. Seemingly, therefore, the quilt was left unfinished by its original maker, and rediscovered and finished decades later.

86 in. wide by 96 in. long
Probably made by a Boyce or Adams family member
Laurens County, South Carolina
14 stitches per inch
83.33 Gift of Mrs. Louise Moseley Heaton in honor of Mrs. Richard Denny Shelby, President General 1980-1983

Framed Medallion Quilt
About 1825-35
105 in. wide by 104 in. long
Made by a member of the Gillam Family
Greenwood County, South Carolina
7 stitches per inch
87.10 Gift of Mrs. Don M. Mayer

Both this quilt and the previous one create their individual look through use of the fabric to the best advantage. The Boyce family quilt cuts up the chintz and spreads it out on a white background. This example sets off the same center with row after row of flamboyantly patterned fabric, efficiently using minimum yardage of expensive fabric. Requiring only basic sewing to connect the strips, it creates a stunning, elegant and fashionable bedspread.

"Mr. Audubon has been upwards of twenty years engaged in this undertaking.…Each plate is ornamented with a drawing of some curious plant of shrub, upon which the bird appears perched, many of which are very beautiful, and have hitherto been wholly unknown to botanists."

"LITERARY INTELLIGENCE," *The Port Folio*, February 1825

Audubon Tree of Life Quilt

1820s

While framed medallions with floral-branching trees and birds in the center are found in quite a number of Maryland and Virginia quilts, the provenance of this particular quilt makes the inclusion of birds especially interesting. The quilt was originally owned by Edward Harris, the close friend, contributor and collaborator of John James Audubon. Their friendship dated back to 1824, close to the probable date of the quilt. Harris was an ornithologist and naturalist in his own right, who supported Audubon in his long struggle to find and document North American bird species. He introduced Audubon to scientific societies and to potential backers for his monumental publication, *Birds of America*. Harris gave Audubon specimens from his own studies and travels to paint, bought him others, and mediated disputes between Audubon and John Bachman, coauthor of *Quadrupeds of North America*. Harris accompanied Audubon and helped to pay for three of his expeditions -- to Labrador in 1833, to the Gulf Coast in 1837 and up the Missouri River in 1843. Audubon acknowledged Harris's help and friendship in his descriptions of the woodpecker, hawk and finch he named after Harris.

The large center medallion, which features a flowering tree composed almost entirely of pieces from one large-scale floral print, on which two large birds perch, is surrounded by three white borders with eight-pointed stars in the corners, bounded by four sawtooth edges. The tree and birds are sewn on in broderie perse style, that is, motifs are cut from a printed textile and appliquéd in a different arrangement. These figures were cut from a 32-inch English block-printed panel printed around the 1780s.

The "teeth" defining the first three frames around the center are made of block-printed flowers and amoeba-like shapes on a red background. The last row of teeth has small geometric figures and pin dots on a brown background. An eight-pointed star anchors each corner, similar to the placement of roundels or studs in wooden frames. The effect is that of a "shadow box" used to frame decorative prints of the era. The first and second sets of stars are Turkey red prints, while the third set has darker brown and black small-figured prints. The eight-pointed stars in the borders are constructed of a different printed cotton in each border: deep pink and white in the first; multicolored pink in the second, and browns in the outermost border. The "teeth" are oriented such that they face to the center of each side, with a larger triangle at the center of each row of teeth. At the corner of each sawtooth row is a square of the same fabric.

The quilting outlines the motifs in the center, then surrounds them with paisley-shaped feathers and flowers. In the three frames, the feathers flow along a curving vine, with half flowers filling in the arches.

Harris's family members made the quilt, according to tradition recounted by the donor. His mother died in 1810 but had five sisters, one of whom was the mother of his first wife, Mary. A family letter of 1826 to Mary from Harris's sister Sarah confirms that both had the fine sewing skills typical of well-to-do women of their day. Thus while no evidence exists of the quiltmaker's name, there are many candidates among Harris's tight-knit and interrelated family of sister, aunts and first cousins. Harris married another first cousin many years after Mary's death in 1831, but she was too young at the time the quilt was made to have participated. The quilt was always known in the family as "the Audubon quilt."

84-1/2 in. wide by 87 in. long
Maker Unknown
Owned by Edward Harris
Probably made in New Jersey
9-11 stitches per inch
96.69 Gift of Dorothy L. Darrach in honor of Edward Harris

"I suppose Lydia is quilting?" said she to Mrs. Emsworth.

"No," replied Mrs. Emsworth, smiling, "we always do our quilting in the summer when the days are long."

—"THE QUAKER GIRL," by Miss Leslie, Ladies' Garland and Family Wreath Embracing Tales, Sketches, Incidents, History, February 1843

Norris Family
GENEALOGY QUILT

1846

Mary Norris of Hagerstown in western Maryland received this "memento of affection from her Grandmother Mary Norris," as the inscription reads, on February 12, 1846. The Norrises were a wealthy Quaker family in Baltimore. The younger Mary's grandmother and namesake filled the large (61 by 63 inches) center medallion with inked inscriptions and decoration. This included two elaborate floral wreaths, one inside the other, with the space between them filled with inked medallions enclosing genealogical information on the Norris family and young Mary's mother's parents. Between the medallions, four chintz flower sprigs are appliquéd.

The elder Mary made this elaborate and elegant quilt, with no fewer than ten concentric borders using printed cottons imported from England. Maryland quilts benefited from access to the port of Baltimore's constant influx of the latest styles in fabrics. Some of the flowers in the Norris quilt are the same ones seen in Anna Catherine Garnhart's eagle quilt from Frederick, Maryland (page 32), while the Greek key borders are quite similar to Mary Tayloe Lloyd Key's quilt (page 94) and identical to that used in two quilts at the Baltimore Museum of Art. These coincidences reinforce the popularity and widespread availability of certain styles of fabrics.

The borders are arranged in not quite symmetrical pairs of sawtooth borders, appliquéd chain-like designs and appliquéd floral sprays. Sawtooth borders were often used in Maryland framed medallion quilts. The edges are bound with green woven tape. Norris used several different quilting designs throughout. Feathering and floral motifs intermingle with hanging diamonds, clamshell and parallel lines.

The DAR Museum also owns a needlework landscape, "A View Near Exeter" made by Rebecca Rooker, sister of Mary Rooker Norris. It serves as a reminder that women in any given family were engaged in many forms of needlework throughout their lives, sometimes reinterpreting similar motifs such as flowers, vines, trees and others from one medium to another.

---

104 in. wide by 102.5 in. long
Made by Mary Rooker Norris
Harford County, Maryland
9 stitches per inch
86.143 Friends of the Museum Purchase

Eliza McKee's Appliqué Vine Quilt

1836

Eliza Shyrock McKee appliquéd her quilt with the date 1836 and her married initials E.M., at the bottom of the quilt. This is a bit confusing, since she was not married until 1838. Her husband Robert had moved from their native Hagerstown, Maryland to Missouri in May 1837, but returned to marry Eliza on May 10, 1838. They moved to Missouri, apparently very soon after their marriage. Perhaps Eliza and Robert were already engaged when he left for Missouri the first time, and she was making the quilt for her trousseau as early as 1836. Or possibly, the initials and date were added afterward.

The flowers in Eliza's central medallion baskets and corners manage to appear both tidy and exuberant, and her vines undulate perfectly across each side and around corners. The overall effect is energetic yet orderly, and very aesthetically pleasing. The use of tulips in the center baskets recalls German folk art motifs seen in Eliza's region, where German settlers' arts and crafts, introduced in the colonial period and still in use in the 19th century, influenced decorative arts among non-German residents.

Remarkably, the vines, a mere half-inch wide, are entirely cut on the straight grain. This would have made the fabric strips extraordinarily difficult to manipulate in their curvilinear meanderings, yet they are expertly managed and sewn. The quilting is a mixture of outline, clamshell, diagonals and feather designs. Together, Eliza's appliqué and quilting create a graceful and charming quilt.

92 in. wide by 101 in. long
Made by Eliza McKee
Washington County, Maryland
12 stitches per inch
96.1   Gift of the Clark County (Missouri) Chapter, NSDAR

Tree of Life COUNTERPANE

1816

"Her talents were properly cultivated: she was well-informed in history, geography, music, and drawing, particularly the two latter, of which and elegant needle-work, she was the perfect mistress; and their best parlor, which was usually termed Eliza's tea-room, was ornamented with the productions of her needle and pencil."

—"EDGAR AND ELIZA," *The Intellectual Regale*, April 1815

This exuberant counterpane was the creation of Sarah Eugenia Coker of Laurens County, in the western part of South Carolina. Family history states that this counterpane was made for Sarah's 1816 marriage to her cousin, William C. Gary, and that the design was her own. Although created at the height of popularity of neoclassical design, the spread exhibits none of the characteristics of this style. Symmetry, balance, restraint…none of these tenets of neoclassicism is to be found here. Instead, an engagingly energetic and highly stylized design is executed in a myriad of embroidery stitches. There is more influence of earlier, exotic, Jacobean-era designs typical of 18th century crewelwork than of neoclassical or romantic naturalism.

The style of this exuberant design derives from English embroidery tradition, and the floral vines emerging from the center urn are as much a Tree of Life design as a flower basket. The flowers and leaves are highly stylized and executed in a somewhat naïve manner. Decorative effects achieved with variations in stitches were the goal, rather than botanical accuracy. Sarah used a large variety of stitches, including outline; broad overcast and Cretan stitch; buttonhole, open buttonhole and buttonhole eyelet; bullion; satin; and French knots.

Three-ply cotton yarn is used for the embroidery on a plainwoven cotton. In the center is a spray of flowers and foliage issuing forth from an urn. Four corner bouquets emerge from narrow, cornucopia-like vases, with what appear to be twining ribbons connecting them, creating an inner border. The outer border is a meandering vine executed in a wide satin stitch bordered with herringbone stitch, with flowers and foliage as offshoots, and primitive bows and tassels in each corner. Two rather comical birds perch on the outer vine at upper left and middle-right; the one on the left has a small heart embroidered within it and holds a worm in its mouth.

A fringe is applied to the bottom and just one side of the counterpane. This fringe has two components: a 2-inch wide knitted band, very possibly made by Sarah, and a 1-inch wide, probably professionally-made woven fringe, connected by herringbone stitch to the knitted band. The fringe does not appear to be lost from the third side; rather, it is knitted in precisely this length, ending just shy of the corner. Was this perhaps intended for a bed in a corner, where fringe would not be seen?

69 in. wide by 84 in. long
Made by Sarah Eugenia Coker Gary (1787-1881)
Laurens County, South Carolina
69.215   Gift of Dorothy Sweeny Castigiola

Hearts and Swags Counterpane

About 1820-35

This whitework counterpane appears to be made of hundreds and hundreds of small, tufted white cotton balls—what we would call "pom-poms." Upon close examination, however, the 1/2-inch-diameter balls appear to have been made from the same thick cotton cord that was used in the bows and tassels in the border. This upholstery cord is couched with whipstitches to create a ropelike texture for the bows and tassels, which punctuate the swags. To create the "pom-poms," the cord would have been firmly stitched down at close intervals, and then cut between each stitch. The ends would then unravel to create a tufted ball. Many candlewick spreads use cut embroidery thread to create a continuous, chenille-like pile design, but this one fools the eye to look like hundreds of distinct balls.

The counterpane uses many motifs popular in the decorative arts of the time, including its abstract octagonal medallion in the center; grape clusters and a meandering grapevine; and the outer border of large swags and tassels. The grapes are embroidered in heavily padded satin stitch and stem stitch, while the vine is made of the same upholstery cord that forms the "pom-poms" and the knots and tassels in the swag border. A thinner, two-ply cotton, candlewick roving is used to embroider the grapes' stems and tendrils. The "pom-poms" are used to create the medallion, hearts, swags and tassel ends, and the zigzag border around the edge of the counterpane. A 5-inch deep hand-knotted, tassel-edged fringe finishes the bottom and side edges.

Nancy Tower Safford of Springfield, Vermont was the maker of this counterpane. Family history related that she made it with her only daughter, Rebecca, who was born in the late 1820s. The date assigned is based on stylistic characteristics, but if the family history is correct, the counterpane must date to at least the mid-1830s.

92 in. wide by 101.75 in. long
Made by Nancy Tower Safford (1787-1854)
Made in Springfield, Vermont
86.84 *Gift of Anne L. Holmes*

"To complete the furniture of the bed, there is laid over it, in the day time, a counterpane of muslin, with a show fringe, and sometimes worked with flowers – a gaudy covering to the misery which lies buried beneath, 'like roses o'er a sepulcher.'"

"MEMORANDA," *American Ladies' Magazine*, November 1836

French Knot Counterpane

1827

> *"Sleep is prevented by an unpleasant degree of either heat or cold, and in this ever-varying climate, where often 'in one monstrous day all seasons mix,' delicate thermometrical persons will derive much comfort from keeping a counterpane in reserve for an additional covering in very cold weather: when some extra clothing is needful by night, as a great coat is by day."*
> —"THE ART OF INVIGORATING AND PROLONGING LIFE," *The Atheneum*, April 1, 1823.

This charming counterpane is embroidered entirely in French knots, using a two-ply cotton roving on a lozenge or diaper-weave cotton. The flower basket and the swag border were two of the most popular decorative motifs of the first half of the 19th century, not only in quilts but in furnishings and other decorative arts as well. The basket's weave is suggested by its flat trellis design; three flowers surrounded by leaves fill the basket. An oval, simple-chain border surrounds the basket and defines a center medallion. A vine with flowers matching the basket's surrounds the medallion, bordered by a diamond-shaped chain. The outer border is a large swag with ribbons and tassels. In the space between each swag is a flower similar to the rest. The counterpane's corners are square at the top and rounded at the bottom; the edge is finished with a 2-1/2-inch woven fringe on three sides.

The donor identified the maker, whose initials L.B. are near the top under the swag, as a distant relation, Lydia Barker, believed to be from New York State. Unfortunately the donor gave no more details, and no connection between the donor and any of the several Lydia Barkers to be found in New York around this time has yet been found.

85.5 in. wide by 94 in. long
Made by Lydia Barker
Possibly made in New York
47.141   Gift of Grace E. Rogers in memory of Helen Baldwin Rogers

"The Mount Vernon Ladies' Association of the Union, of which Miss Ann Pamela Cunningham, of South Carolina is Regent, have executed their patriotic work with a success and spirit which put the exertions of our own sex to the blush."

—Article 2 – No Title, "Well Done for the Ladies," *Christian Inquirer*, April 16, 1859

DAR MUSEUM

Medallion and Hearts
WHITEWORK QUILT

1830s

Ann Pamela Cunningham is famed for leading the battle to save Mount Vernon for the nation beginning in the 1850s. But as a young woman, she created this handsome quilt. At the age of seventeen in about 1833, Ann Pamela injured her spine in a fall from a horse, and became a lifelong invalid. Perhaps she made, or at least began, her quilt before her accident; or perhaps she made it to fill otherwise dull and idle hours at home.

Ann Pamela's quilt uses exquisitely drawn and stuffed floral and grape motifs, but arranges them within a framework that calls architectural moldings to mind. The center medallion has two twelve-lobed borders and a central oval; stuffed-work flowers fill all the fields within the medallion. Surrounding the medallion is a large field of double-diamond quilting, edged with a meandering, running, feather-variation border. Inside each corner of this border is a stuffed flower with a stem and two graceful leaves, set against clamshell quilting. Carnations, grapes and various flowers bloom improbably on a meandering vine in the next border. The corners of this border, too, are set off with a quarter-medallion with a single flower inside each corner. Outside these, large hearts are flanked on each side by simple, gracefully curving leaves. Lastly, two narrow, linear borders, each a row of stuffed hearts nestled inside each other, frame a feather vine variation with more flowers. A 2-1/2-inch woven fringe edges the sides and bottom, and a woven tape completes the top. The background quilting changes with each border: small-scale hanging grid begins in the center medallion; double diamonds in the main center field with clamshells in the corners; hanging grid reappears behind the first floral vine; and diagonal quilting offsets the last vine. French knots add detailing and textural interest on some of the flowers.

The extensive use of hearts—in the outer two borders and in the interior corners—would normally make us think of love and marriage, and speculate that this was a wedding quilt. However, as Ann Pamela never married, the hearts were most likely used because they were a decorative motif popular at the time.

98 in. wide by 103 in. long
Made by Ann Pamela Cunningham (1816-1875)
Made in Laurens County, South Carolina
9-11 stitches per inch
54.160   Gift of Floride Cunningham Burney,
Ann Pamela Cunningham Chapter

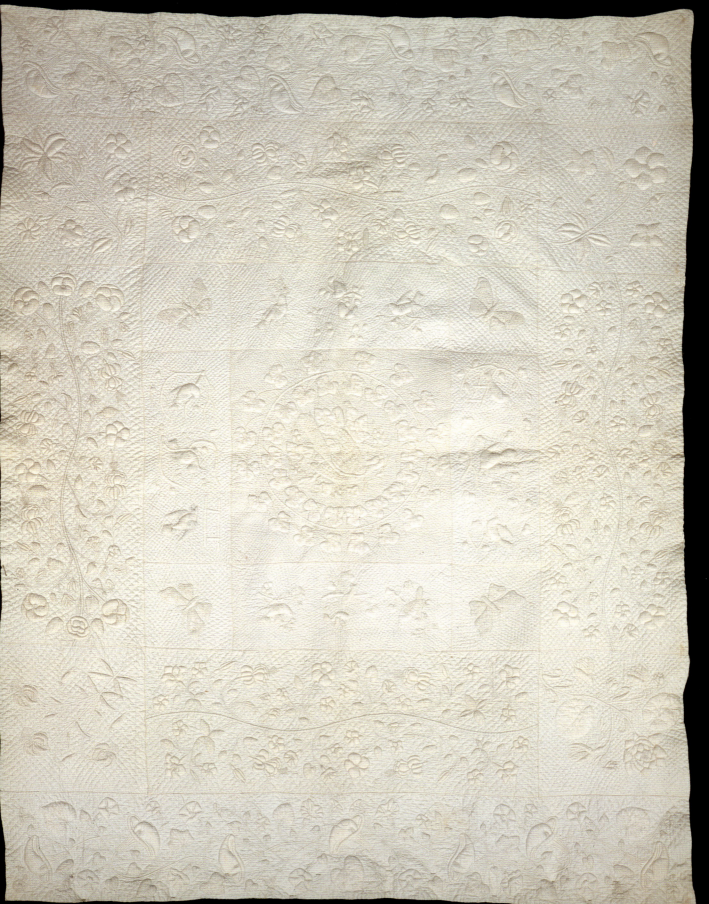

Embroidered and Stuffed Whitework Quilt

1840s

This whitework quilt, larger than cradle size but too small for a bed, exhibits beautiful and striking combinations of stuffed work with white embroidery outlining and detailing the flowers. The quilt is constructed somewhat unusually, with nineteen small panels. These were clearly made separately, as their diagonal background quilting does not match up at any point. Likewise, the stuffed-work designs in each panel are self-contained, not connecting or relating to their adjoining pieces. A center medallion is surrounded by two borders, each of which has corner squares and separate side pieces. A final panel stretches across the width of the quilt at both the top and the bottom.

The center square is embroidered with a bird perched on a branch surrounded by an ivy wreath. It is surrounded by four corner squares, each with a butterfly, and four side panels with more perching birds and ivy sprigs. The second border's side pieces, and the final top and bottom panels, are embellished with graceful and abundant floral vines, on which a variety of flowers bloom. These include calla, tiger and water lilies; morning glories; pansies; and fuchsias. The corner squares of the second border have more flowers in bouquets. All the flowers and butterflies have white embroidery outlining their petals adding texture and detail. With its combination of highly stuffed motifs, embroidered details, and the diagonally quilted background, the quilt is a visual feast and a display of masterful needlework.

The maker of this beautiful quilt was Sarah Varick Hewlett, whose family was of Dutch heritage in Long Island, New York. Sarah and her husband George Hewlett, who was from another old New York family, moved from Long Island to the Finger Lake region of New York sometime between 1840 and 1848. The use in this quilt of six-ply quilting thread, which was not available until after 1840, helps date the quilt. But as we cannot pin down the date of the Hewletts' move upstate, we cannot be sure in what part of New York it was made.

49 in. wide by 69-1/2 in. long
Made by Sarah Varick Hewlett (1807-1867)
Made in Suffolk or Yates County, New York
10 stitches per inch
87.43   Gift of Helen Jones

"The Committee on Art and Industrial Exhibits of the Women's Centennial Union desire to urge upon the women artists and artisans of New York and other States the importance of sending to them at once for inspection and approval such specimens of their work as my be suitable for exhibition in the Women's Pavilion at Philadelphia, and credible to the women of our country."

—"ART NOTE," *The Ladies' Repository: A Monthly Periodical Devoted to Literature, Art,* June 1876

Four-block Eagle Quilt

About 1876

Although we don't know who made this quilt, its patriotic theme makes it especially appropriate for the DAR Museum collection. Not only are the four eagles taken from the United States seal, but the center wreath is known as a Presidential wreath, surely a conscious choice by the quiltmaker.

American eagle motifs enjoyed several surges of popularity in both quilts and the decorative arts in general, first in the Federal era and especially around the time of the War of 1812; again during the Civil War in the Northern states; and nationwide around the time of the Centennial in the 1870s. It seems likely that this quilt dates to the time of the Centennial. The four-block design of American eagles facing the center on the diagonal is seen in quite a number of quilts in almost exactly identical format, with variations in the center motif. While no design source has been identified, it seems likely that a common source must have existed for such close resemblances to exist. Of the surviving quilts with this design that have any known history, all come from Pennsylvania; thus we can guess that this one, too, may have originated there.

The eagles and wreath are made from the same pale yellow cotton, making it difficult to guess their original color. A green seems likely for the wreath, but would the eagles have been green? A slightly darker shade of yellow is used for the shields. It is difficult to guess whether both these fabrics have faded similarly from two shades of green, or whether the quiltmaker chose an unconventional color scheme. The eagles have no feet, nor are any feet indicated by either embroidery or quilting—perhaps another quirk on the part of the maker.

The eagles' heads, torsos and their shields are quilted in rows of clamshells. While these are common quilting background motifs, in this context they manage to suggest overlapping feathers. More natural textural effects are seen in the wings and tails, which outline more realistic arrangement of bird feathers. The remainder of the quilt is elaborately quilted. Sunflowers are placed under each eagle wing, with small hearts and a variety of abstract leaves and other decorative motifs filling in much of the rest of the white areas. The wreath has several rows of outline quilting both inside and outside.

A feather border outlines the seam of each of the four center blocks, and another meanders along the outer border of the quilt, with chevrons above and below it.

PHOTO RETOUCHED TO SHOW COLOR AS IT MAY HAVE ORIGINALLY APPEARED.

85 in. wide by 88 in. long
Maker Unknown
Possibly made in Pennsylvania
9-10 stitches per inch
87.95.229   Gift of Albemarle (Virginia) Chapter in memory of Mildred C. Brown

"Maybe, this winter she has decided to make one of those truly beautiful sewed on quilts. If it's her first one she will choose one of the simpler designs like the 'Washington Vase,' for instance. She will be very painstaking with the fine sewing and it will be a success. Emboldened by this she may undertake one of the more elaborate designs, which calls for 5 or 6 times as much fine sewing. If she does, it will, most likely, be time she has finished it. If she really sticks to it and works conscientiously, it will certainly be worth all her effort and her 'Whig Rose,' or 'Cactus' or 'Prince's Feather,' will be something to "show" to people when they drop in."

—"THE HOME AND FAMILY" by Florance M Albright Mrs Ivy J Neff, *Indiana Farmer's Guide*, October 23, 1920

Louvica Houchins's
Princess Feather Quilt

1839

The whirling plumes of the Princess Feather design were a popular motif for appliqué in the mid-19th century. This example was made in 1839 by Louvica Houchins for her granddaughter and namesake. The name Princess Feather has often been identified as a corruption of Prince's Feather, and linked with the feather plumes of the insignia of the Prince of Wales. However, a recent study of quilts made in this design suggests that a more likely source was the amaranth family of plants[1]. These were popular in American gardens in the 19th century, and "prince's feather" was one of its many common names. The feathery fronds of the amaranth plant, commonly red or deep pink and sometimes green, are recognizably similar to the plumes found in Prince's Feather quilts—and Princess Feather is an easily understood variation on the name. Louvica Houchins's gift to her granddaughter features many of the most common features of Princess Feather quilts. These include the red and green plumes on a white ground, four quadrant layout without sashing, use of eight alternating red and green plumes, and inclusion of a border.

Louvica's quilt also has the characteristic energy and sense of movement of Princess Feather quilts. The curve of the feathers make the blocks appear to spin clockwise. This whirling effect is enhanced by the visual contrast of the alternating colors of red and green. Instead of simply marking the center "stem" of each feather, Louvica used three reverse appliqué half circles placed in alternating directions, which add to the sense of movement. At the center of each circle of plumes is a red star, with pink printed cotton circles at its center and at each point.

The border is unusual, and deceptively simple. Instead of a meandering curvilinear vine, Louvica chose an angular zigzag border with alternating red and green plumes between zigzags. And instead of turning the corners and making the plumes alternate colors continuously, she gave each side its own pattern, which is mirrored in reverse colors on the opposite side. The energetic angularity of the border is softened not only by the plumes, but by the crescent-shaped flowers between two leaves under the zigzags. Pink printed cotton circles like those in the center stars appear at the corner of each zig and zag.

The background quilting consists entirely of feather motifs. Solid red binding matching the appliqués has become worn and frayed, and in some areas has been covered with a heavier dark maroon red cotton. At some point the quilt won a second place ribbon in the "Most Elaborate Border" class, probably at a county fair. Unfortunately, no one in the family recorded where this accolade took place.

---

80 in. wide by 89 in. long
Made by Louvica Houchins (1788-1863)
Made in Logan County, Illinois
47.147   Gift of Mrs. Charles F. Trader

---

1 Carol Williams Gebel, "The Princess Feather: Exploring a Quilt Design," *Uncoverings* 28 (2007), 129-164.

Margaret McClelland's MAZE QUILT

1850s

This uniquely designed quilt's elaborate maze pattern has inspired much speculation about not only its source, but the reason for the quiltmaker's choice of such an unusual design. Many medieval churches and cathedrals had labyrinth designs on their floors, which were used for spiritual exercises, pilgrims walking (or, penitentially, edging along on their knees) the long circuitous route to the center. Some churches today continue this practice. McClelland's design is quite similar to the design at Amiens Cathedral in France. It's important to note, however, that the quilt's design is a maze, not a labyrinth. Labyrinths have just one, circuitous route to the center; mazes have many false turns and dead ends. Regardless of this distinction, would medieval cathedral floors have been known to her, and why would a Virginian Episcopalian put a medieval Catholic symbol on her quilt?

The Greek myth of the minotaur contained in the maze at Crete, where the legendary hero Theseus slew him, is another possible source, though only indirectly. No design for the legendary maze was ever proposed, and the remains of the Cretan palace at Knossos were not discovered by archaeologists until 1878 (with no labyrinth other than the confusing plan of the palace itself).

Recent research into Margaret Cabell's family and their home in Nelson County, Virginia, has suggested another source of the quilt's design. Margaret's childhood home, "Union Hill," had a boxwood maze in the gardens. A family member recalled much later that its design was that of a butterfly. It was also said to have been similar to a maze at Patrick Henry's nearby estate, Red Hill. Henry was a family friend, whose son married the quiltmaker's daughter Elvira. Although the butterfly designs cannot have been a direct inspiration, with two such mazes so well know to the quiltmaker, it seems less of a surprise she constructed her own.

Turkey red plain cotton strips are appliquéd to a plain white cotton ground, forming an octagonal maze. Additional strips decorate the corners to form a tessellated border called "Walls of Troy," a configuration inspired by and named for the fortifications around the classical city. At the center is a letter "C," probably for Margaret's family name, Cabell. The quilt is backed with plain white cotton, and bound back to front on three sides, with applied binding on the fourth. The only quilting outlines the design.

83.5 in. wide by 79.5 in. long
Made by Margaret Cabell McClelland (1785-1863)
Made in Nelson County, Virginia
8-9 stitches per inch
87.87   Gift of Margaret Willis

Mary Sneed's Texas Baskets

1850s

According to family history, Mary Deloach Sneed made this quilt in Texas with one of the first treadle sewing machines brought there. Mary and her husband, her first cousin George Washington Sneed, moved from their native Tennessee to Texas for George's health in 1850. Sadly, George died the following year.

Mary's quilt consists of twelve nearly identical blocks set on point with overflowing fruit baskets in stuffed appliqué, alternating with plain white cotton blocks, which have indeed been machine quilted. The fruit baskets fill their blocks almost to bursting, and oranges, apples, and red grapes overflow from them. The baskets' brown printed cotton's design features ribbonlike stripes seeming to weave in and out of each other, creating a cheater cloth for the fruit baskets. The effect is enhanced by the stripes' having been outline quilted, so that they appear to actually be woven.

The fruit is made from solid glazed cottons, stuffed to add depth to the design. A narrow green soutache braid is used to create the grape clusters' tendrils, and a wider green tape forms the grape leaves' stems at the upper corners. Green embroidery thread outlines the leaves' veins. Mary Sneed's fruit baskets resemble those found on quilts of the period on the East Coast, but hers have a more limited, and darker, color palette, which gives them added visual impact. Enhancing this further, dark green glazed cotton is used as a background for the fruits immediately above the basket; only the leaves and grape clusters stand out against a white background.

The white blocks have grid quilting on point— done on the machine Mary was so proud of. The grid's squares are a mere 1/4 inch in size: no quilter would want to do that by hand. But the miraculous sewing machine allowed speedy rows of stitching. Here, Mary was celebrating, even showing off, her ownership of this new invention. It may well have been one of the first in her part of Texas. Initially expensive, the sewing machine was cleverly marketed by competitive manufacturers, and soon was priced within the reach of a large portion of the middle class.

The sewing machine was hailed as the liberator of women, freeing them from the miles of tedious sewing required for every household. In Mary's time, every sheet, towel, tablecloth, and other piece of household linen had to be hand-sewn, as did nearly all the clothing. Hardly anything was available ready-made. The sewing machine sped up dreary household sewing tasks— freeing women, if they chose, to do decorative sewing. It was no coincidence that women's dresses began to sport miles of decorative trim shortly after the sewing machine's popularization. Likewise, Mary Sneed chose to sew row upon perfectly-aligned row of grid quilting in her white blocks.

The quilting was done on the blocks before they were sewn together, and an additional backing of white glazed cotton was put on the quilt. This was then not quilted, but tied at the corners of the blocks. There is no quilting on the appliqué blocks; the fruit and basket take up all available space.

82 in. wide by 94-1/2 in. long
Made by Mary Deloach Sneed (1807-1905)
Made in Waco, Texas
92.1 Gift of Martha Hunt in honor of the Descendants of Mary Deloach and George Washington Sneed

"But by-and-by she moved to another house, and where do you suppose? Under the great flower-basket quilt that was stretched upon the frame, and you haven't an idea unless you have tried it, what a lovely house that makes. There Polly gathered her dishes, and the cat, and a rag baby, and was happy as a queen."

—"GRANDMOTHER'S CURTAINS" by Mary L. B. Branch, *The Youth's Companion*, February 1, 1877

DAR MUSEUM

Mary King's Appliqué Quilt

1850s

Red and green appliqué floral quilts from the mid-19th century abound, but this one rises to a higher level of artistry and charm. It was made by Mary King, whose name is appliquéd—twice—near the center, "Mary. King." The punctuation seems to lend emphasis and suggest determination, not unlike Mercy Deuel's counterpane (page 140). Interestingly, however, Mary King, who married David Harper shortly after 1860, was more properly known as Verlinda Mary, and appears as Verlinda or Linnie in census records, leaving us to wonder why she styled herself as Mary on her quilt. (Perhaps its brevity was appealing.)

Whatever the confusion over the name, Mary King has both followed the contemporary trend for red and green florals, and struck out on her own to create an individual design. Though living in northwestern Pennsylvania, her motifs show the influence of Eastern Pennsylvanian German ("Dutch") folk art, such as the feathered pinwheel in the center, the stylized floral baskets, and the birds facing each other (perched on the floral vine border). Her own twist is the addition of four pairs of adult birds—of strange shape and indeterminate species—bending over nests to feed their young, which form a border around the central pinwheel. Outside the birds, floral baskets, large and small, alternate with green leafy fronds (essentially repeats of the pinwheels); the final border is a floral vine, as seen in so many red and green floral quilts. This, however, is more complex and individual than most, with its three alternating floral and berry sprigs, and its birds perching along the upper crests of the vine, irregularly spaced around the quilt. Pink and blue fabrics are used in a few places in addition to the primary colors of red and green, providing accents that add to rather than detract from the effect of the whole. In all, Mary's quilt has energy, originality and charm that tell us more about who she was than any census record.

89 in. wide by 97 in. long
Made by Verlinda Mary King Harper (1837-1931)
Allegheny County, Pennsylvania
7-9 stitches per inch
2005.25   Gift of Ama J. McElhaney Chambers

Verlinda Mary King Harper, about 1895, with her granddaughter Peg Harper.

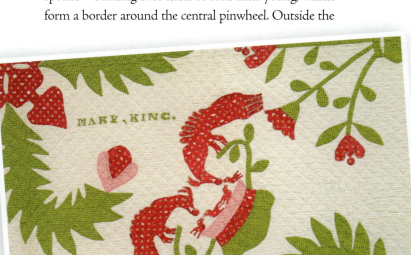

"Should the colour fade in washing (that is the red and green) it will be necessary to give the goods a drop or two or oil of vitriol in cold water after rinsing; this stays the colours."

—"DYING, &C.," *Maine Farmer and Journal of the Useful Arts,* May 4, 1839

Ruth Jean Carter's BERRIES AND REEL QUILT

1850s

Nine appliquéd reel designs set on point, bordered by a vigorously meandering vine, create a quilt full of movement. The quilt's current colors are red and dark tan, but the latter would have been a vivid green originally. Like so many green dyes, this one has proved unstable over time. However, in its heyday, the quilt would have had the popular complementary color combination of red and green, as seen in the retouched photo.

Each 17-inch square block includes an eight-petaled poinsettia, with floral buds extending from every other petal on the horizontal and vertical axes. Between these motifs are stems covered with berries, whirling clockwise and giving the quilt its dynamic effect. The sense of movement is enhanced by the height of the border's vine stem, which meanders energetically up and down as it "grows" from the lower left corner. Unlike border vines in some of our other quilts in this book, this one does not emerge from a vase or flower pot. Its berries and flowers repeat the motifs in the center blocks.

The white squares and triangles all are quilted with three exotic stylized flowers in a vase. The flowers are filled with tiny scallop quilting, and their upper edge is a half-row of feathering. Offsetting the curvilinear appliqué designs, the background quilting in both white and appliqué blocks is vertical lines a quarter inch apart. The border has diagonal quilting.

Family history recorded that this quilt was made by Ruth Jean Carr, who was the donor's great-great-grandmother. Genealogical research into the donor's family reveals that this great-great-grandmother's maiden name was actually Ruth Jean Carter, whose daughter Amanda married William Carr in 1853. Possibly the quilt was made by Ruth as a gift for Amanda's wedding. The family lived in Jefferson County in northeastern Ohio.

---

91 in. wide by 95 in. long
Probably made by Ruth Jean Carter (1796-1878)
Made in Jefferson County, Ohio
12-14 stitches per inch
99.23.1   Gift of Jean Henderson Douglas

PHOTO RETOUCHED TO SHOW TRUE COLOR BEFORE FADING.

Margaret McMath's Tulip Quilt

About 1850

"I fancy what is lost in time is gained in power; that is, power to boast over a neighbor who actually quilted a "Philadelphia pavement" in five weeks, while their "Tulip quilt" occupied just six weeks and four days." These precious articles are kept folded up in the most careful manner; it would not do to use them for fear of soiling, for the first touch of soap suds would make them look like a flower garden after a June frost."

—"QUILTING FRAMES," *Michigan Farmer*, June 1, 1854

We know little about Margaret Jane Ford, but her quilt reveals clues of a complex personality. Sixteen large [17 inches square] blocks separated by 5-3/4-inch sashing contain stylized sprays of red and yellow tulips. The main stems create a strong diagonal across each block on which three evenly spaced flowers dart like bright arrows. All of the blocks are pointing toward the same direction, giving a rigid formality to the design. A very different look could have been achieved by altering the placement of the blocks or by setting them all on point. Lest her arrangement seem too severe, she gave a slight curve to the cross branches that fill the block to the corners topped by more of the same flowers. These angular bouquets are composed of fabrics that seem solid from a distance but reveal themselves as cheerful small prints upon closer examination.

The quilting continues the diagonal theme with parallel lines stitched behind the appliqués and diagonal lines stitched slanting in the opposite direction into the sashing. The four corners of the quilt deviate from the formula. Each one has the shape of a hand, clearly traced from life, quilted into it. Whether they are Margaret's own hands or those of family or friends is unknown.

Margaret lived all her life in Rockbridge County, Virginia, on the East side of the Shenandoah Valley; but her choice of pattern shows an appreciation of designs we normally associate with the Pennsylvania Dutch. She married John McMath in 1850, and this quilt dates from the same time period, though we have no information that it commemorates that event. The quilt was donated to the museum by the great-granddaughter of the quiltmaker.

The rest of the quilting is quite plain. The blocks and border have diagonal quilting, the sashing and border being done in the opposite direction from the blocks. The sides and top have an applied binding, and the top is self-bound.

89 in. wide by 95 in. long
Made by Margaret Ford McMath (1832-1917)
Rockbridge County, Virginia
10 stitches per inch
78.29 *Gift of Harriet Booker Lamb honoring her maternal ancestors*

"Many a curious device, and many a beautiful picture is to be traced in the well selected and well arranged colors in piecing quilts. Some spend their ingenuity in imitating flowers – a pink, a rose, a sunflower, or a myrtle wreath – some prefer a cluster of bright colors, and form a flower-pot, or a wreath of various vines, and some try to imitate the stars above and piece beautiful bright patches, and set them in white or blue, in imitation of the upper sphere."

—"MY PATCHWORK QUILT," by Mary Hall, *Arthur's Home Magazine*, March 1863

Garden Maze Floral Wreath Appliqué Quilt

About 1860

The most striking aspect of this quilt is the contrast between the cheddar yellow of the sashing and the navy blue background. The effect is softened somewhat by the use of the white fabric to complete the garden maze design that frames the floral appliqué blocks. Instead of piecing the Xs at the intersections, the maker simplified the construction of the effect by appliquéing them. The four outermost corners are missing this detail.

The quilt is designed to be viewed from all directions equally. The center block is composed of four floral elements placed in a balanced arrangement around a center bow, shaped rigidly with loops and ties in polarity. The blocks that form the center cross of this nine-block quilt place the same flowers as the center on circular wreaths. The outer four corners mimic the wreaths but are actually made of separate elements, the tendrils of the floral sprays whimsically sewn down in slightly varying shapes. The outer border of a brown print seems dull by comparison but may have been brighter when the quilt was constructed. If one imagines the oil lamp or candlelight in use when the quilt was created, the choices of color and contrast become more understandable.

The garden motif continues in the quilting. All the appliqués are emphasized with outline quilting and the blue background has leaf shapes stitched into it. The sashing is filled with a quilted leafy vine. The outer border is simply quilted in a diamond grid.

The inscription on the quilt, "M.A. Baden 150 years old," was not made by the quiltmaker. The quilt was not 150 years old until after its donation to the museum, and Baden is not the maker's name but a very small town in Maryland close to where she lived. Martha Ann Turner was born Martha Ann Gibbons and married John Turner in 1817. They lived on the west side of the Patuxent River in the southern part of Prince George's County, a county now mostly taken over by suburbs of Washington, DC. In her lifetime, the entire county was farmland, and her husband John Turner was a prosperous planter, with twenty-eight slaves and real estate worth $13,000—then a considerable sum—in 1850. John's position in the community played a minor role in a major part of American history. After President Abraham Lincoln's assassination, Dr. Samuel Mudd was tried for conspiracy in the crime because he had treated John Wilkes Booth. Booth had broken a leg leaping to the stage of Ford's Theater and while escaping through the Maryland countryside, sought and received medical assistance from Dr. Mudd. John Turner testified as a character witness in Dr. Mudd's defense, stating Mudd was not a Southern sympathizer and had helped Booth for purely humanitarian reasons, not political ones. Alas, John Turner's testimony was not enough to prevent Mudd's conviction.

100 inches square
Made by Martha Ann Gibbons Turner (1792-1868)
Made in Prince George's County, Maryland
6-8 stitches per inch
87.69 Gift of Mary J. Child

Marie Webster
DOGWOOD QUILT

1932

This is one of the few 20th century quilts in the DAR Museum's collections. No historic American quilt collection could be without a sample of this iconic quilt designer's work. Marie Webster's designs and writing were to a great extent responsible for the resurgence of interest in quilting in the early 20th century. She began publishing articles on old quilts, and adapting old appliqué patterns for new, in *Ladies' Home Journal* in 1911-12. Transfer patterns for some of Webster's designs—not the full kits she would later offer—were available from the magazine for fifteen cents. Her first book, *Quilts: Their Story and How to Make Them* followed in 1915. In 1921, Webster founded her Practical Patchwork Company, which marketed kits for her quilt designs. The appliqué shapes and quilting designs were pre-printed on cloth that was included in the kit.

Webster was one of the first to sell quilt kits in this way, and in so doing showed remarkable business acumen. She tapped into the market she had herself helped to create by reviving interest in quilting, aiming for a wide and not necessarily highly skilled customer base. While experienced needlewomen could also enjoy them, her quilt kits were also easy enough for modern women—in general much less skilled in sewing than their foremothers had been—to assemble. At the same time, Webster's designs combined a feeling for American floral appliqué traditions and a modern aesthetic. The quilt designs were influenced by the Art Nouveau and Arts and Crafts movements. Both these design movements loved nature and floral and foliage designs, which Webster pared down to their essentials in the relative simplicity required in bold appliqué designs. Her colors likewise catered to the prevailing taste for soft pastels.

This quilt's pattern name was "Dogwood," and was first published in *Ladies' Home Journal* in January, 1912. The article enthused that it "offers another good choice in flower design and one of unusual delicacy and coloring. The full-grown blossoms on the green background reminds us delightfully of the beauty of trees and flowers in early spring." The design was also featured as color plate 7 in *Quilts: Their Story and How to Make Them* as well as being sold by Webster's pattern company later on. Its green background, a popular color at the time known as Nile green,

> "Every now and then there comes to light one of these old quilts of the most exquisite loveliness, in which the needlework is almost painful in its exactness. Such treasures are worthy of study and imitation, and are deserving of careful preservation for the inspiration of future generations of quilters."
>
> —*Quilts, Their Story and How to Make Them,* by Marie D. Webster, 1916

is typical of the soft colors preferred in early 20th century design. Dogwood blossoms are simplified into a symmetrical quatrefoil. Their yellow stamens are represented by a pale yellow circle at the center. The petals are given their characteristic indentation at the edge with pink blush peeking out at the undersides of the petals represented by small patches of pale pink. The four-color palette creates a simple and effective design.

The quilt is constructed in twenty-two blocks, each 11 inches square, set on-point, around a central square block with a "wreath" of partial dogwood blossoms and leaves. Inside this center medallion is a quilted wreath of blossoms with grid quilting inside it. Each of the blocks making up the main field of the design has an X formed by five dogwood blossoms, with four dogwood blossoms quilted in the corners. Together the blocks create a floral lattice pattern. This is edged with a border of simplified dogwood trees, each with two blossoms placed such that they continue the line of the lattice with diagonal background quilting. The darker green scalloped edge, which finishes the quilt, suggests the old swags so popular in mid-19th century appliqué quilts.

This example of Webster's design was made by Martha Louisa Moffett, née Pogue. She lived most of her life near her parent's farm south of Fresno in southern California; in the 1930 census, she was living in Pasadena near Los Angeles with her two unmarried daughters. She was known as Lydia, and signed her quilt with this name and the date 1932. She pieced the blocks by machine, and did the appliqué and quilting by hand. Lydia's sister recalled in the family history she published that their mother had been a quilter, and that "in the evenings Father used to help her quilt. He could quilt as beautifully as Mother, I think. One or two quilts in the family bear his initials, where he worked them."[1] Since he died in 1907, he could not have helped with this quilt, but this memoir tells us that Lydia came from a family tradition of quilting, surely learning it at her mother's knee, and had no need of the ease of a modern quilt kit. Nevertheless, she chose the design, likely for its visual appeal, and created a handsome quilt.

---

77 in. wide by 90 in. long
Designed by Marie Webster (1859-1956)
Made by Martha Louisa Pogue "Lydia" Moffett (1862-1934)
Made in Pasadena, California
9 stitches per inch
99.49   Gift of Jane N. and Florence Montgomery Coughran in memory of Elise and Mildred Moffett

[1] Eva Pogue Kirkman, *Family History of J.W.C. Pogue, 1st* (Exeter, CA: privately printed, 1945), p. 32.

"Mary Simon" Style Baltimore Album Quilt Top

1846

In the mid-1840s, a new style of quilt emerged in Baltimore and was copied in surrounding counties of Maryland. It is the style we now call the Baltimore Album quilt. Made of appliqué squares assembled in rows, sometimes with a border, the Baltimore Album reached a pinnacle of design excellence seldom equaled in quilt history. The genre has been the subject of decades of research into the squares' designs and origins, and yet there is still much we do not know. The student of American quilt history may pick up a book or catalog on Baltimore quilts from the last thirty years and find several different theories about the albums' designs and designers.[1] The most elaborate style, as seen in this quilt's twenty-five squares, has been variously attributed to Mary Evans, an unnamed "Designer I," and most recently, Mary Simon.

Mary Simon was mentioned by Hannah Trimble (in the entry quoted on page 80) as "The lady who cut & basted these handsome quilts,"[2] and the two quilts Hannah saw that day can be identified as specific surviving Baltimore albums in the style of Designer I. After the discovery of Hannah's diary, all Designer I squares were ascribed to Mary Simon, the German-born wife of a carpet weaver who did indeed live on Chestnut Street. Immigration records show that Mary arrived in America after the earliest dated blocks in the Designer I style were made, which seems to indicate that Mary Simon was simply cutting and basting the fabrics according to someone else's design and preparing the squares for sale. The DAR's quilt top was purchased at the time that Mary Simon was believed to be responsible for the design and manufacture of this style of square, so we have always called it the Mary Simon quilt.

The topic of who made Baltimore album quilts, and how they were made and distributed, continues to be the subject of ongoing research and heated scholarly debate. At the time of Katzenburg's and Goldsborough's work, about fifty Baltimore albums were known; in the succeeding thirty years, dozens more have come to light, causing some early attributions to be reassessed. Clearly, with such a large body of work, no one woman could be responsible for sewing all the squares of any given design style. The sheer volume of squares in various styles, often identical and using identical fabrics, strongly supports the notion that many squares were commercially produced as sort of early kits, "cut & basted" by someone like Mary Simon, and sewn, assembled and signed by the many women of Baltimore, from shoemakers' and laborers' wives to upper middle-class ladies.

Our "Mary Simon" quilt top is both exciting and frustrating to the progress of Baltimore album quilt studies. It contains twenty-five classic Designer I/Mary Simon style squares, many of which can be found in almost identical form in several other Designer I quilts in other collections. It can be dated

---

1 Jennifer Goldsborough gives an extensive summary of BAQ studies in her article "An Album of Baltimore Quilt Studies," *Uncoverings* 15 (1994), 73-110.
2 Hannah Mary Trimble, Diary, Manuscripts Division, Maryland Historical Society Library, MS2517, 1 Feb. 1850. Quoted in Goldsborough, op. cit., p. 97.

firmly because of an inked inscription on the back, which reads "Trophy of Love 1846." But while the squares themselves represent the pinnacle of the most elaborate design style in Baltimore albums, we have absolutely no history associated with the quilt to give us further clues. We know only that it was owned by the family of a man who lived in Massachusetts, a salesman whose territory included Baltimore. Did he purchase the quilt? Did a colleague or friend in Baltimore give it to him? We will never know. We lack even any signatures on the blocks to research for family and community connections to each other and to other quilts.

We are left to admire the sophisticated design, skillful execution and thoughtful arrangement of the twenty-five squares. At the center, an American eagle flies with a garland in its beak and a flag in its talons. The eagle is made from a wood-grain printed fabric in blue, which is characteristic of these "Simon" squares and which gives texture suggestive of feathers to the eagle. Four flower baskets anchor the corner of the squares surrounding the eagle. Flanking the eagle are the Baltimore Merchants' Exchange building and the U.S. Capitol as it appeared before its second dome was added. Below the eagle is Baltimore's monument to George Washington, a major city landmark. In the outer ring of squares are found many more of the typical "Mary Simon" blocks, including the bird carrying the book inscribed "ALBUM"-- which makes clear the connection between these quilts and ladies' autograph friendship album books.

Each of these squares contains dozens of pieces, layered as if in a collage to create depth and detail. Many of the DAR quilt's designs are found in nearly identical format, even with exactly the same fabrics, in several other Baltimore albums (the DAR's Andrew Jackson quilt on page 82, for example, contains a fruit epergne). The DAR's "Mary Simon" quilt is extraordinary because each of its squares represents the most elaborate version of any of its twins in other quilts. Even without signatures or history, this Baltimore album stands out as an unparalleled example of its genre.

86 in. wide by 84 in. long
Unknown maker
Made in Baltimore, Maryland
98.31   Friends of the Museum Purchase, Purchased with funds from the estate of Opal C. Backus

"…went to Mrs. Williams in Exeter St. to see a quilt which was being exhibited…it was surpassingly beautiful. The star spangled banner & holy bible—an eagle with flowers issuing out of the Liberty cap formed the center. Around it were…baskets of flowers, a great variety of wreaths &c &c…then out to Mrs. Simon's in Chesnut St. The lady who cut & basted these handsome quilts—saw some pretty squares."

—Hannah Mary Trimble's Diary, 1850

95 in. wide by 98 in. long
Made in Baltimore, Maryland
12-16 stitches per inch
87.68   Gift of Catherine T. Winter

Andrew Jackson
COMMEMORATIVE ALBUM QUILT

1845-47

The central block of this Baltimore album quilt is an appliquéd heart enclosing an inscription attributed to President Andrew Jackson. "The Blessings of Government, Like the dew of Heaven, Should be equally dispersed on the Rich and the Poor," it states, a political sentiment typical of Jackson's Era of Good Feelings and his extension of voting rights to all free white men. (Previously, only men of property could vote; black men, and women, had decades more to wait.) "Victory at New Orleans January 8th 1815" and "Andrew Jackson Heart" are inscribed above the quotation. Beneath it is the name A.I.W. Jackson.

This date led to an early misattribution of the quilt to 1815. But as Dr. William Rush Dunton noted when he studied this quilt in his book *Old Quilts*, this more logically refers to the battle of New Orleans at which Andrew Jackson won his fame. Research into the signers of other blocks indicates that the quilt must date between 1845 and 1847. President Jackson died in 1845. Ann Carson's block is signed with her maiden name, so the quilt predates her 1847 marriage. And we know it was made for William and Betsey Harper, who married in 1848.

The Andrew I.W. Jackson whose name is on the center square (no relation to President Jackson) was a prominent Baltimore citizen active in the labor movement of the 1830s, supporting "Jacksonian ideals of individual liberty and equal economic opportunity."[2] Thus it makes sense that the Jacksonian quote and tribute are found in his square. Many other signers of blocks, both men and women, were members of the Methodist Episcopal Church of Baltimore. It is also notable that several of the men who signed the quilt are listed in the census as shoemakers, and one was a printer. These professions were at the forefront of the labor movement, forming the first local trade unions in Baltimore.

The quilt's five rows of five squares are surrounded by an appliqué floral vine border. The squares represent the work of several different designers. Many are more elaborate professional blocks; others are homemade copies of these styles. Most of the flowers are stuffed. Many roses are edged with pink wool blanket-stitched embroidery, with additional embroidered details in wool, silk and metallic thread. The arrangement of the designs is not perfectly symmetrical, but eight floral baskets or urns surround the center, while eight wreaths, three of them classic examples of what is now known as the Presidential Wreath, dominate the outer row. The border is not perfectly continuous; the vine ends at three corners, a clever way of avoiding the difficulty of making an undulating vine arrive at the perfect turning point at the corners. The border has diagonal background quilting in the upper and lower areas, but tiny clamshell quilting in the middle. The squares have diagonal background quilting, the direction alternating from square to square, with a feather wreath at the corners where four blocks meet.

---

1 William Rush Dunton, *Old Quilts*. Catonsville (MD): privately printed, 1946.

2 Virginia Vis, "Presidential Wreath and the Jackson Quilt," *Blanket Statements* Issue 102 (Winter 2010-11), pp. 1, 3-5. Virginia has done exhaustive research on the genealogy and background history of this quilt, and this entry owes everything to her work. Her research on each square and its signer is most fully documented in the quilt's file at the DAR Museum, but each signer is identified and discussed in her article.

103 inches square
Probably made by Ruth Penn (b. 1807)
Made in Baltimore, Maryland
10-11 stitches per inch
92.172   Gift of Jane Disharoon Bunting, Ann

Penn Family Baltimore Album Quilt

1850s

A curious inscription is quilted at the center of this classic Baltimore album quilt: SAMOHT ROFPRBQ P PENN. The letters themselves are not backwards (except for the F), but they are arranged backwards—partially—and are abbreviated—also in part. Knowing that Ruth Penn made this quilt for her son Thomas gives us a key to this cryptic inscription. If you begin with the Q and work left, it seems that Q B R P stands for "Quilted by Ruth Penn" and the remainder reads "For Thomas." Then you must return to the Q and proceed to the right for the rest of his name, "P. Penn." What on earth was Ruth Penn doing? Was she dyslexic? Eccentric? We'll never know. In fact, we don't know a great deal about Ruth or her son. In 1850 Ruth, apparently a widow, was the head of the household in Baltimore City with her 20-year-old son Thomas, who was listed as a "combmaker," and a younger brother and sister.

What we can tell is that Ruth, living in Baltimore, followed the then-current fashion for beautiful floral appliqué blocks in the heyday of the Baltimore album quilt. The uniformity of the design style of the blocks, and the skill with which they have been pieced, which far outweighs Ruth's stitching skills, support the current understanding of Baltimore album blocks as having been sold as pre-cut and sometimes basted kits. Ruth Penn chose to assemble a quilt entirely composed of 21-inch squares by the same designer. She placed four blocks with flower urns at the center, surrounded them with twelve floral wreaths, and finished the whole off with a simple swag border. The wreaths vary in design, with anywhere from four to eight flowers. Seven wreaths enclose smaller urns; several also have added embroidered details. The color scheme, unsurprisingly, is red and green, typical of mid-century appliqués and of many Baltimore albums in particular. The quilting is eccentric and irregular. Ruth seems to have begun to do rather large-scale clamshell quilting, which appears in several squares, but each time she abandons this in favor of large-scale, clumsily drawn, stylized feather-and-leaf motifs. The peculiar inscription is quilted in running stitch in the center. Two large anchors are found near the top and along the right edge. Hearts are also scattered about. The most charming detail is the outline of a small child's hand near the upper right border. Whose? We'll never know.

All squares but one are signed; somewhat unusually, whereas many album quilts contain a mixture of men's and women's names, here all the names appear to be women's. (Several are illegible because of the deterioration of the fabric from the ink.) Two names are stamped; one is repeated in cross-stitch in two squares. Unfortunately, many of the names which can still be read are too common in Baltimore to allow us to confidently pin down their identities. Thus we cannot know how they were connected to the Penns by blood or other ties. But this seems of little import compared to the handsome effect of sixteen beautiful floral album squares arranged pleasingly in this classic Baltimore album quilt.

"An album quilt is a very pretty idea. A lady gives the size of the square she wishes to each of her lady friends, who are willing to contribute to her quilt. They make a square according to their own taste, putting a white piece in the centre, on which they write their name. Every lady's autograph adorns her own square. An old lady in Charlestown showed me one in which there were one hundred squares, and all the contributors excepting twelve were dead. The quilt itself belonged to her mother, and was more than sixty years old."

"PATCHWORK," by Ellen Lindsay, *Godey's Lady's Book and Magazine*, February 1857

Quaker Album Quilt

Probably 1847

Preparing this book has spurred us to do new research on quilts we've had for a while, and this is a case where we've been able to enrich our knowledge of a quilt, and in so doing, revise our thoughts about its origins. This album quilt descended through the family of Thomas Sykes, a Quaker in southern New Jersey, and it was thought that the quilt was made for him. But examining the signatures and researching their family connections has led us to reconsider.

Thomas Sykes was in his seventies in the 1840s when this quilt was made—an unlikely candidate for a quilt presentation. His name appears on the quilt, along with three of his four children and many other relations. His daughter Edith's name is missing, however; and as she married in 1847, it seems entirely possible that the quilt was made for this occasion. We know it cannot have been made after 1847, as a cousin who married that year signed her maiden name. Edith was nearly 30 when she married Earl Gibbs and had two children before her husband died in the mid-1850s. The quilt passed down through her granddaughter and namesake Edith Sykes Gibbs, born just weeks after the elder Edith died in 1888.

The format of the quilt is typical of Quaker album quilts made in New Jersey in the mid-19th century. These albums have blocks, which may be pieced or appliquéd, and are arranged on-point with narrow sashing in between. The Sykes quilt follows this format, with most of its forty-one squares being pieced. Some squares are identical or extremely similar; usually these are signed by people with the same surname, either husband and wife, sisters, or presumed close relatives. The squares have been arranged thoughtfully with similar designs placed symmetrically. There is also balance, if not symmetry, in the placement of the red and white geometrics, which dominate the design. The outer edge's triangles are made from the same tan and blue print as the pieced sashing, framing and unifying the whole. The cotton prints include a great many Turkey reds, some greens and a few browns and blues. The backing is a handsome blue and white striped floral cotton. In all, it forms a masterful design and a testament to close family ties in a Quaker community.

105 in. wide by 107-1/2 in. long
Made by members of the Sykes and Earl family
Probably made for Edith Sykes Gibbs (1808-1888)
Made in Burlington County, New Jersey
7-8 stitches per inch
94.23 Gift of Dorothy Truitt in honor of Mrs. Billie Joe Lovett, Librarian General

DAR MUSEUM

Fish Family Chintz Album Quilt

1843

Album quilts such as these were popular in Trenton, New Jersey and nearby Philadelphia in the early to mid-1840s. In contrast to the Baltimore-style albums, these feature much smaller squares with a single, large-scale, printed cotton motif appliquéd on each one. These albums derive from the tradition of chintz appliqué. Several of these distinctive albums are found in museum collections across the country. Three of them—the DAR's, the Denver Art Museum's, and the one at Lincoln, Nebraska's International Quilt Study Center—are closely linked, sharing both signatures and fabrics. Recent research by quilt scholar Carolyn Ducey on this trio has caused us to reevaluate what we thought we knew about our quilt.[1]

We have always thought that our quilt was made by Emma Fish as a gift to her Aunt Eliza Moore, whose name is inscribed in the center medallion. The IQSC quilt was believed to be the work of Emma's mother as a present to her daughter-in-law (Emmeline Howell, who married Emma's brother Jonathan Fish about 1840); both their names appear in the center medallion. But after Ducey's exhaustive analysis of the fabrics and names on these two quilts and the third, she poses a convincing new theory. It now seems more likely that all three quilts were made under Aunt Eliza's supervision, one by Emma and one by her sister-in-law Emmeline, the third by Emmeline's sister-in-law (and cousin) Anna Perrine. The overlap in fabrics and signatures strongly suggests that the fabrics were bought together and shared among the girls; their interconnected families signed the squares, with variations on each quilt, but the most overlapping on Emmeline's and Emma's. Aunt Eliza Moore, who never married, was found in later censuses living with Emma's father Benjamin after his widowhood, or with his son Asa; clearly she had close ties to her sister's family. Perhaps in 1842-3 she was visiting and embarked on this sewing project with her niece and two other girls of the extended family. Aunt Eliza's name at the center of Emma's quilt thus reflects her involvement and probable close emotional tie to Emma, not her ownership of the quilt.

Emma's quilt is made of a grid of eighty-one squares; a central medallion of a floral wreath enclosing a peacock takes up the equivalent of nine squares. Most

> "This is indeed an Album fair, A rich memento, wrought with care;
> A page of memory's dearest lines, Where art, combined with beauty, shines.
> And when, as on through life we tread, We turn and gaze upon this spread,
> We'll engrave upon our grateful hearts The names of those who formed its parts."
>
> —"TO THE QUILT," *The Universalist Union*, 1845

of the 9-inch squares contain a single flower or spray, with a few containing wreaths or other compositions of several motifs. There is diagonal quilting in the background of the center medallion and the border, but the squares have only an outline 1/4 inch inside the seam of each square.

The fabrics are all the latest and finest imported English chintzes that would have been readily available from the fashionable port city of Philadelphia, just across the river from Trenton. Emma's father Benjamin Fish was a wealthy man, with real and personal estate valued at $150,000 in the 1860 census (the equivalent of well over a million dollars today). Thus, the Fish girls could easily afford the high-end fabrics fresh off the ships from Europe. Except for several squares with peacocks or stylized Indian-style florals imitating paisley shawls, Emma preferred full-blown roses in large sprigs or wreaths; the other two quilts contain somewhat more botanical variety.

The signatures on Emma's quilt date mostly to December 1842 to February 1843. Some of the dates are identical to those on the other two quilts. Many squares are signed Trenton, New Jersey, with a smattering of squares signed Philadelphia and nearby New Jersey towns. Signers of Emma's quilt include her parents, her brothers and their wives, and Fish uncles and aunts. Emma's mother's Moore relations and several Howells (Emmeline's family) are also included. The Moore, Howell and Fish families had been connected by marriage as early as the mid-18th century. The similarity of the quilts and the repetition of names across the three quilts testify to the interconnectedness of these families in their community.

94 in. wide by 104 in. long
Probably made by Eliza Moore (1797-1880) and
Emma Maria Fish (1825-after 1910)
Made in Trenton, New Jersey
6-7 stitches per inch
5254   Gift of Mrs. C. Edward Murray

1 Carolyn K. Ducey, "Chintz Appliqué Albums: Memory and Meaning in Mid-nineteenth Century Quilts of the Delaware River Valley" (Ph.D. Diss., University of Nebraska, 2010), chapter 3 (31-62), appendices A-G.

Log Cabin PATCHWORK

Late 19th century

The unknown maker of this Log Cabin tablecloth arranged her colors expertly. Not only do the colors radiate beautifully in the Barn Raising variation, but the strips in each log get darker from the center to the outer edge, giving each square the illusion of depth. The juxtaposition of complementary colors—red and green, yellow and purple—further intensifies the energy of the composition. Radiating squares, shaded strips, and contrasting colors interact to make this textile virtually pulsate before your eyes.

The center of each of the sixty-four squares is black silk velvet. Although red centers are commonly associated with log cabin designs, black centers are quite common as well. The silks used in the patchwork are mostly solid, but also include plaids and stripes. Satins and taffetas predominate. The backing is cotton, and instead of a binding, a braided wine-red silk cord and tassels adorn the corners.

Like most Log Cabins, this one has neither filling nor quilting. This was not intended to provide warmth on a bed; rather, its fancy silks, small size and cord and tassels proclaim it as a tabletop for a late Victorian period home, a showy piece of needlework to adorn a parlor and testify to the domestic skills of the lady or daughter of the house.

64 in. wide by 65 in. long
Unknown Maker
Made in the United States
92.175   Gift of Carolyn C. Marshall in memory of Mary Olive Marshall

---

"Have you seen anything prettier than log cabin pattern for a silk quilt, Sister Huldah?" asked Mrs. Phillips after a short silence. "I have heard there are new patterns, but they haven't got around to Smyrna yet. You coming from a big city so, must have seen a good deal."

"A silk quilt? No," said Huldah, again taking up the old magazine. "That's a pity. Why I don't recollect a bride in Smyrna these five years who hasn't had some sort of a silk quilt. Some of 'em even went down to the paper mill and picked over the rags to get silk pieces."

Elizabeth Cumings, "STORY OF AN ARTIST," in *Music: A Monthly Magazine*, 1891

Mrs. Francis Scott Key's Counterpane

About 1840-45

"Patchwork may be made in various forms as stars, triangles, diamonds, waves, stripes, squares &c. The outside border should be four long strips of calico, all of the same sort and not cut into patches. The dark and light calico should all be properly contrasted in arranging patchwork."

—Fancy Needlework, 1830-1846

Mary Lloyd Key was the wife of Francis Scott Key, who wrote "The Star-Spangled Banner." He was a lawyer in Georgetown, in the District of Columbia, for most of his adult life, but returned to his native Maryland before his death in 1843. Mary Key remained in Maryland after his death; this unquilted patchwork counterpane may have been made in either place. It dates to decades after the writing of our national anthem, yet its family history is intriguing. The outer edge is a printed cotton border in a Greek key design, surely chosen as a reference to the family name.

Mary Key's design is a framed medallion with a center square medallion, a second frame on point, and two additional borders. Each border is defined by a printed cotton band, and is filled with alternating white and printed cotton triangles. The center and corners of the center border feature masterful 32-pointed Mariner's compasses. The outer border is divided by fabric bands into five triangles per side. Overall, there are nearly 3900 triangles throughout the quilt. Although the arrangement of their colors appears random, most rows have a limited number of symmetrically arranged prints. Mary clearly spent time thinking carefully about the layout of her many printed cottons.

The cutting and piecing of so many triangles is testimony to the Keys' social standing and material comfort. Handsome printed cottons in many colors would have been specially purchased for the project, which would have required many leisure hours. Whether living in Washington or Baltimore, Mary would have had access to the latest printed cottons imported from Europe. Baltimore was a major port, and merchants in Washington DC bought from dealers there as well. No matter where she was, Mary Tayloe Lloyd Key created a bedspread that testifies even now to her taste and skill.

109 inches square
Made by Mary Tayloe Lloyd Key (1784-1859)
Made in Washington, DC or Baltimore, Maryland
4037 Gift of Frank F. Greenawalt in memory of Maud Lipscomb Greenawalt

"… so when Julia became absorbed in the idea of a piece of needle work more elaborate and difficult than anything that had been accomplished in the village — something that required art and genius, a good eye for form and colors, to execute well — I became fascinated with the idea of piecing a quilt, known by the old ladies, who are connoisseurs in such matters, as a 'rising sun.' Now this title when applied to a counterpane consists of red, green, yellow, blue and white calico, cut into infinitesimal atoms sewed together and forming a star-like centre which radiates over a white ground in rays of purple, azure, pink, and every variation of rainbow colors. In short, it is a sort of homeopathic principle scientifically embodied in a patchwork quilt."

—"THE PATCH-WORK QUILT" by Mrs. Ann S. Stephens, *Graham's Lady's and Gentlemen's Magazine*, January 1844

Sarah Kyle's Star Quilt

1839

Sarah Kyle made this quilt at the age of twenty-two, a few years before her marriage to David Caldwell. Family history states that her mother and sister helped her make it in preparation for her eventual marriage. But as Sarah was the last of eleven children, including three sisters who may have been at home in 1839 when the quilt was made, we can't be sure which sister helped—or whether, more likely, they all did. The quilt went with Sarah's daughter, Jemima, when her family moved to Texas shortly after 1900. Sarah's great-granddaughter donated not only the quilt, but a friendship album with locks of hair of family members and friends. From this not uncommon practice of saving hair mementoes, we have an uncommon piece of information about a quiltmaker: Sarah had dark chestnut-brown hair.

The quilt features five Stars of Bethlehem in a cheerful array of red, pink, green, dark and teal blue and tan diamonds. The red, blue, tan and green cottons are multicolored roller prints that would have been very stylish and new at the time. Between the stars are squares with red eight-pointed stars matching the center of the larger stars, surrounded by quilted feather wreaths. On each edge of the quilt between the stars are two partial Bethlehem stars, as if to continue the pattern created by the five central stars. In the small square on the bottom of the quilt, just in from the left corner, Sarah inscribed her quilt "Sarah, H, Kyle November, 2 AD, 1839." in green thread.

Sarah's quilting is fairly elaborate. Her stars are quilted with parallel diagonals, and the triangles around the edge have double grid quilting. The large squares and small square corner blocks all have close-set rows of echo quilting. The corner blocks feature pinwheels, and most of the rest of the small squares have flowers and vases, all of which are distinctly influenced by Pennsylvania Dutch designs. Sarah's father emigrated from Ireland in the 1780s, and her mother was from an Anglo-American family, but the motifs testify to the pervasiveness of the designs of southeastern Pennsylvania.

Sarah Harper Kyle, about 1860

102 in. wide by 101 in. long
Made by Sarah Harper Kyle (1819-1898)
Made in Newville, Cumberland County, Pennsylvania
6-7 stitches per inch
95.44   Gift of Elizabeth Osteen

Hannah Wallis Miller's
Mosaic Quilt

About 1840-45

"Charlotte hurried on; and her thoughts soon returned to the idea of the splendid radiating star which she designed for the centre piece of her counterpane. While she was arranging the different patterns, and forming the alterations of light and shade, her interest continued nearly unabated; but when she came to the practical part, of sewing piece to piece with unvarying sameness, as usual, it began to flag. She sighed several times, and cast many disconsolate thoughts at the endless formation of hexagons and octagons, before she indulged any distinct idea of relinquishing her task: at length, however, it did forcibly occur to her, that, after all she was not obliged to go on with it; and that really, patch-work was a thing that was better done by degrees, when one happens to want a job, than to be finished all at once."

—"BUSY IDLENESS," *The Guardian, or Youth's Religious Instructor*, August 1, 1820

Hannah Wallis Miller's quilt is a veritable sample book of printed cottons of about 1840. Each hexagon is cut with a motif from the fabric centered on it, what we now call "fussy cut." Hexagon quilts, made with paper templates, are one of the oldest patchwork designs. European and American examples date back to the 18th century. *Godey's Lady's Book's* first article on patchwork in 1835 offered instructions for hexagon or "honeycomb" patterns. Hannah's quilt does not retain its paper templates.

Hannah's hexagons are arranged in what is now called Martha Washington's Flower Garden, although that modern term would never have been used by Hannah herself; she would have called it "honeycomb" or "mosaic." The arrangement is a series of diamond-shaped motifs with a center hexagon surrounded by two rows of eight and then sixteen hexagons. These diamond-shaped clusters are accentuated by rows of white hexagons that outline them. A single red hexagon appears where six diamonds' points meet. As a result, these clusters appear to form a series of six-pointed stars. The quilt is edged with a printed paisley border and bound with a woven tape. The backing is a roller-printed cotton, and a thin cotton filling is quilted primarily by outlining the hexagons.

Hannah Wallis Miller was the daughter of a land baron in Colonial Pennsylvania, Samuel Wallis. Samuel had a colorful career in the American Revolution. Although a Quaker, he joined a unit of the Pennsylvania Militia. But it was not until the 20th century that it was discovered that he had also been one of Benedict Arnold's spies for the British. Hannah was born in the middle of her father's spying career, yet appears to have led a conventional and blameless life. The creation of this beautiful quilt should atone for any political sins of her father. The quilt was passed down through the generations until Hannah's great-great granddaughters donated it to the DAR.

98-5/8 inches square
Made by Hannah Wallis Miller (1781-1859)
Made in Philadelphia, Pennsylvania
8-9 stitches per inch
88.65.1   Gift of Jane and Mary Osborne in memory of their mother, Helena Cady Osborne

Mildred Fox's Bethlehem Star Quilt

About 1880

Without family history, this boldly colored, eight-sided star on black might be thought to be from the Amish or Mennonite community. We know that the maker, Mildred Matilda Buckner Fox, was not Mennonite; but clearly the Mennonite aesthetic was not restricted to that community, but influenced quilters further afield. There were Mennonites in several areas of Missouri, although none close to Paris, where Mildred Matilda lived.

Seven solid-color cottons are used in the star, and five in the diamond border (the light pink appears only in the border, while the gold and olive green appear only in the star). As with many Lone or Bethlehem star designs, the arrangement of the colors in the radiating rows of diamonds creates an energetic optical effect. This is dramatically enhanced by the use of the black background, against which the colors "pop."

A printed brown cotton backing, wool braid binding and wool filling complete the quilt. The star's diamonds are outline quilted, while the background has a diamond grid and the borders have diagonal quilting.

The DAR collection includes a second quilt by Matilda, a silk hexagon design, also donated by her granddaughter.

79 inches square
Made by Mildred Matilda Buckner Fox (1817-1907)
Made in Paris, Missouri
8 stitches per inch
46.67   Gift of Mrs. Clara C. Bristor

> " 'Glorious!' exclaimed Kitty Moulton, dashing in among a party of girls who were sewing minute patches of bright-colored calico into a quilt, and wasting time and thread sufficient to have purchased half a dozen more beautiful and more serviceable ones."
>
> —"SUNLIGHT FROM SHADOW" by William H Bushnell, *Ballou's Monthly Magazine*, April 1880

DAR MUSEUM

"Yes, there is the PATCHWORK QUILT! Looking to the uninterested observer like a miscellaneous collection of odd bits and ends of calico, but to me it is a precious reliquary of past treasures; a storehouse of valuables, almost destitute of intrinsic worth; a herbarium of withered flowers; a bound volume of hieroglyphics, each of which is a key to some painful or pleasant remembrance, a symbol of – but, ah, I am poetizing and spiritualizing over my 'patchwork quilt.'"

—"THE PATCHWORK QUILT," *The Lowell Offering*, September 1845

Blazing Star Wool Quilt

1840s

This striking wool quilt has a romantic but unverifiable history. It is said to have been made from an old Revolutionary War uniform belonging to Mrs. Strough's ancestor, who may have fought with General Herkimer in New York during the Revolution. (The date of 1840s is suggested by the backing fabrics, printed cottons which date to that decade.) However, although the fabrics are uniform-weight, experts on military uniforms have pointed out that red was not extensively used by the Continental Army—so having enough red to make this quilt is questionable. It's even more questionable whether Herkimer's troops had uniforms at all. It has been suggested that if they are indeed from uniforms, it may be from later militia uniforms. The red is of the sort often used in both men and women's cloaks, both military and civilian, so perhaps a grain of truth to the family history is here: an ancestor of the quiltmaker could have had a red cloak, which he used in the Revolution.

All this speculation and debate is unlikely to ever be resolved, but whatever the origins of the wools used, they make a warm and visually appealing quilt. The primary colors used in a vibrant star design offset by sashing make for a simple and bold effect. Nine blocks, each 22 inches square, are separated by 2-1/2-inch sashing.

The twelve-pointed stars have blue center circles with red curved-edge hexagons inside them. The repeated contrast of red-blue-red adds interest to the simple design. Simple outline quilting is used on the stars' pieces, but each red square surrounding the star has a simple leafy vine surrounding it, quilted in brown (possibly originally black) thread to make it stand out more. The sashing is quilted with grids on point. Two different brown and blue printed cottons in four panels are used in the backing. The filling is rather thin. The same red wool used in the quilt forms a binding, which extends over an inch onto the back and has a pinked binding: a sensible alternative to a turned-under hem made from a thick wool.

67 in. wide by 70 in. long
Made by Mrs. James Strough
Herkimer, New York
5-6 stitches per inch
78.38 Gift of Mrs. Harry E. Boyd in memory of Edna Price Boyd & Harry E. Boyd

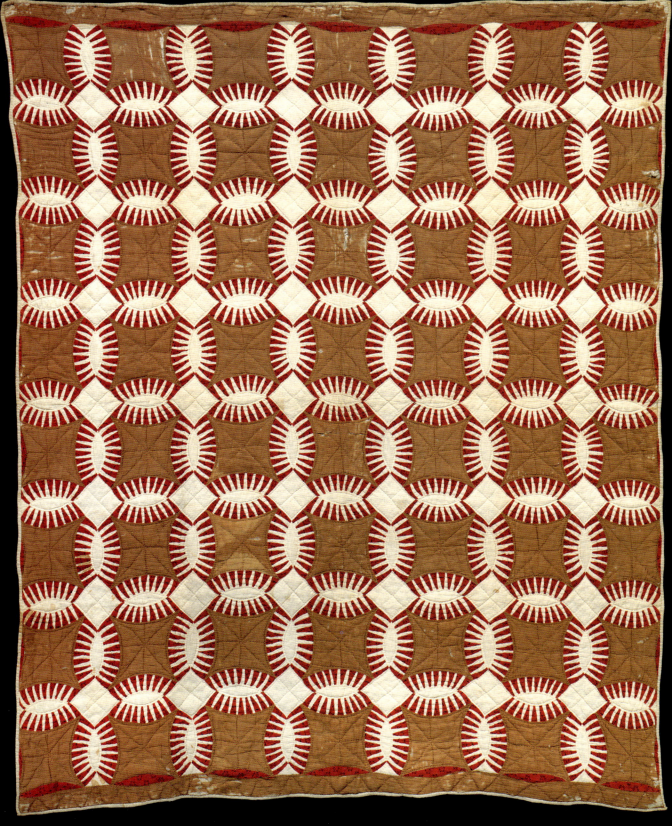

Pickle Dish QUILT

About 1885

> "Why lawsy me! when I was her age I'd cut and pieced seven quilts with my own hands, and when company come, I'd never think, of openin' my mouth."
>
> —"OUR DEB," by Jeff L Harbour, *Ballou's Monthly Magazine*, July 1880

This is recognizable as a "Pickle Dish" design, which was popular in the late 19th century, especially in the South. Like so many familiar quilt patterns, the name can only be documented as far back as the early 20th century quilt revival; but it may well have been in use before then. The design is a variation on overlapping circles, and the pickle dish refers to the almond shape created by the overlap of two circles. Pickle dishes were commonly made in glass and were oval or almond shape. The sharp triangles used in the quilt design evoke the cut glass edging popular in late 19th century glass serving dishes of this kind. It is no surprise that the pickle dish design came into vogue in the late 1800s: it was not until then that tableware became so specialized that there were pieces designed for containing or serving every possible food. The Industrial Revolution made possible the mass-production of affordable goods, and factory-made glass and china were within the reach of a vast cross-section of Americans. Having a great many serving dishes with specialized uses became a sign of material comfort and of gentility.

The simplicity of the brown, red and white piecing on this example gives the quilt a visual vibrancy that is arresting and attractive, but not necessarily restful to sleep under. The red fabric is printed with black abstracted flowers; the brown and white are solids. The pickle dishes' pieces are not true triangles, but taper to a 1/4-inch wide edge—an understandable adaptation of an extraordinarily challenging pattern to cut. The quilting is minimal: a cross and an X divide each brown block; the white squares have a simple X; the top and bottom edges have zigzags. The pickle dishes themselves have two rows of parallel quilting inside each arc.

Although the donor did not know the maker of the quilt, she provided names of her mother, grandmother and great-grandmother, all of whom lived in Pickens County, Alabama. Given its date, it is possible that it was made by either Melissa "Fannie" Williams, born about 1850, or her daughter Minnie Lula (known as Lula), born about 1872. Or, of course, both may have worked on it together. It might well have been made in preparation for the marriage of Lula, the donor's grandmother, to George W. Basinger in 1890.

70 in. wide by 91 in. long
Probably made by Fannie Williams or
Lula Williams Basinger
Probably made in Pickens County, Alabama
4-5 stitches per inch
89.17   Gift of Vernie Blake Schnetzler

Crazy Quilts

Crazy quilts are often less than completely "crazy," and are never actually quilted. The "crazy" element comes from the fanciful, undisciplined arrangement of irregular shapes and sizes of a wide variety of fabrics. More "craziness" is achieved through the addition of embroidered motifs, appliqué and painting. Sometimes decorative ribbons, often souvenirs of fairs and political campaigns, are incorporated. Decorative embroidery in a wide variety of stitches outline the patches, adding more detail.

It seems, however, that although the Victorian aesthetic embraced over-the-top clutter and decorative effects, the Victorian mind could not restrain itself from imposing some order on the crazy's random design. An 1885 journal complained, "the fault of crazy quilts is their craziness. To be really pleasing they should have some design,…which, though very irregular in detail, has yet a general plan, a distinct centerpiece, and a plainly defined border."[1] And in fact, many crazies are "contained crazies," some with a series of bordered blocks in which the random piecing is contained within each square. Instead of quilting, crazies are just backed and sometimes tied. As many of them were foundation-pieced, their thickness would have made quilting prohibitively difficult and unwieldy.

Crazies could be embellished with any sort of motif the maker chose, and perhaps this was part of its appeal: there were no rules about what size, shapes or colors to choose for the patches, and as for the painting or embroidery that adorned each square, "anything goes" was clearly the motto. Popular motifs included birds, butterflies and insects (and arachnids: spiders and their webs enjoyed a curious vogue); flowers and feathers; Kate Greenaway-style children in old-fashioned garb; modern children fishing or playing; and Japanese motifs.

Many of these reflected the influence of the Aesthetic movement in art and design. The Aesthetic style rejected the industrial revolution's mass produced and cluttered styles of decoration. Instead, it embraced both the simple elegance of Japanese arts, and a use of motifs from nature. Peacock feathers and lilies were popular Aesthetic motifs that are often found in crazy quilts.

Japanese vases and paddle-shaped fans are also popular crazy quilt motifs. Japan had recently opened its doors to the West in the late 1860s, after which its wood-block prints and ceramics, imported in large numbers to the West, became enormously popular and influential in Western design. It has been suggested that crazy quilts' irregular design came from Japanese ceramics with a deliberately cracked glaze, called "crazed," meaning irregularly broken up. One of the early names for crazy patchwork was Japanese patchwork, clearly indicating an awareness of inspiration from Japanese design.[2]

Crazy quilts were all the rage in the 1880s and 1890s. Silk crazies are commonest, but wool and cotton ones were also made. Scraps were certainly used, but fabric retailers soon caught on. Realizing that women needed a wide variety of silks for their crazies, they sold bags of scraps just for crazy quilters, as well as pre-embroidered motifs that could be appliquéd. The fad for crazies was declared dead by several humorists in the late 1880s, but in fact it persisted into the first decade of the 20th century. We include here three crazies, and additional details from an assortment of the DAR Museum's twenty-eight crazy quilts.

1 Susan Hayes Ward, "The Homelike House," *The Chautauquan*, vol. 5 (1884-5), p. 462.
2 Penny McMorris, *Crazy Quilts* (New York: E.P. Dutton, 1984), p. 10-11.

Julia Hosford's Crazy Quilt

1880-1900

Julia Hosford combined crazy patchwork with embroidered and appliquéd blocks. The upper left is just one piece of black velvet with couched silver thread embroidered in a large spiderweb—complete with spider and its prey. Other embroideries include Japanese fans, one of which sports peacock feathers, birds and insects. Most remarkable is the square with several lithographed portraits of women. Two appear to be idealized Grecian-style portraits, but the other two are informal smiling faces. The one at the lower right corner of the block has been identified as the then-famous actress, Anna Held.[1] Even then, celebrities were publicized with commercial goods.

A wine-red velvet border edges the crazy with red and yellow herringbone stitching connecting border and blocks. A yellow silk cord is used instead of a binding. The backing is a golden yellow factory-quilted silk satin.

Julia was born in Maine but lived most of her life in Concord, New Hampshire. She also made a handsome log cabin quilt dated 1882, which is also in the museum's collection.

47-1/2 in. wide by 48 in. long
Made by Julia Ann Eastman Hosford (b.1812)
Made in Concord, New Hampshire
85.70 Gift of Mrs. Robert M. Rouse

---

1 Penny McMorris, op. cit., p. 64-5, and letter dated Sept. 16, 1986, to Judith Nordin, Assistant Curator, DAR Museum, in object file for accession no. 85.70.

Anna Hall's Crazy Quilt

About 1840-45

"Henrietta says, 'Now, grandma, you've got to make a crazy quilt; you've made every other sort that ever was heard of.' And she brought me the pieces and showed me how to baste 'em on the square, and said she'd work the fancy stitches around 'em for me. Well. I set there all the mornin' tryin' to fix up that square, and the more I tried, the uglier and crookeder the thing looked. And finally I says: 'Here, child, take your pieces. If I was to make this the way you want me to, they'd be a crazy quilt and a crazy woman, too.'"

—"AUNT JANE'S ALBUM," by Eliza Calvert Hall, *The Cosmopolitan Magazine*, 1900

Anna Hall made this classic crazy quilt in 1888, and another, also in the DAR's collection, in 1894. Both are rectangular with twenty blocks and a velvet border. This one shows a little more variety in its squares: one has pieces radiating out from a center square, and another arranges its pieces like the folds of a fan—a common crazy quilt design. In each square, one to three pieces have been embellished. There are several couched chenille flowers, commonly used on crazies, as well as motifs done in cross-stitch or simple stem stitch. These include a cross-stitched church and pansy in the bottom row, a spiderweb and butterfly, a cat and a dog and various flowers. In the upper left square, Anna embroidered her initials and the date in satin stitch. The embroidery outlining the pieces shows a remarkable variety of type and color—a highlight of crazy quilting. The squares have a cut velvet border on the sides with contrasting blue velvet squares at the corners. A simple maroon-colored cotton forms the backing.

54 in. wide by 65-1/2 in. long
Made by Anna Hall (1858-1936)
Made in Quaker City, Guernsey County, Ohio
92.154.2   Gift of Mr. Don Strouse on behalf of Priscilla Lingo Lamneck

Almira Boggs's
PAINTED CRAZY QUILT

1880-1900

We recognize this as a kind of crazy quilt, yet it does not display the randomly pieced patches that normally define the genre. Instead, it is the sashing, which is pieced in a formation know as Chinese Coin, surrounding the twenty-five painted 8-inch squares of brown taffeta. Painted flowers or other fauna decorate twenty of the blocks. Three blocks are made from a textured velvet whose flowers are more or less outlined with oil paint. Two blocks have a child motif: a boy fishing and a pinafore-clad girl at a gate. The 2-1/2-inch wide sashing has inch-long strips of a variety of silks, including satin, taffeta, faille and figured silks. In the squares where rows of sashing intersect, smaller floral motifs have been painted. The large blocks are all outlined in typical crazy fashion, with a variety of decorative embroidered borders.

The donor believed this to have been made by her ancestor, Almira Boggs. Almira, her husband and their two daughters, Myra age thirty-five and Lilia age thirty, were living in Cambridge, Massachusetts in the 1880 census. Any one or more of the ladies of the house might be responsible for the painting and sewing of the handsome quilt.

58 in. wide by 68-1/2 in. long
Possibly made by Almira Lincoln Boggs (1809-1895)
Possibly made in Cambridge, Massachusetts
76.112   Gift of Mrs. George U. Baylie

"…A very pretty way to utilize scraps, odds and ends of silk, is to make them into blocks for a crazy quilt… Tiny pieces, only inch-square strips, triangles, anything and everything can be utilized. Silk and velvet are the prettiest, and in this day of bright ribbons quite easy to get. On the plain piece in each block may be worked an emblem, embroidered or painted, or all three may be used on one square…"

—May Perrin Goff – The Household: a Cyclopedia of Practical Hints for Modern Homes, 1881

CENTER

DAR MUSEUM

Embroidered Silk
Satin Bedspread

Late 19th century

This exquisitely feminine bedspread was embroidered in Macao, China for the Western market. Macao was settled by Portuguese traders in the 16th century, and remained a Portuguese colony within China until it was returned to Chinese rule in 1999. Silks designed and decorated for the Western market were prized imports in Europe and America for centuries, and embroidered silk bedspreads in this style were made in Macao at the end of the 19th century. This would have been a fashionable and luxurious choice for a bedroom, reflecting the latest trends in interior design at the time. Light colors, delicate furnishings and a general air of simple elegance and restraint were the watchwords of a new style that was supplanting the dark and cluttered interiors of the mid-Victorian period. A bedspread such as this would have graced a room in this new aesthetic. The Tilghmans who owned this spread were a branch of one of the oldest families in Maryland, dating back to the 17th century.

The bedspread combines the aesthetics of East and West. European-style flower bouquets appear in the center medallion, the corner of the main field, and around the border. They are combined with very Chinese-looking birds sprinkled throughout the field, flying between smaller flowers, and with Chinese-style butterflies flitting among the flowers in the outer border. Blue and pink are the predominant colors, and a pink and blue embroidered ribbon winds its way from bouquet to bouquet in the border, lending an energetic rhythm to an otherwise very orderly arrangement. All is executed in satin stitch on a rich, creamy colored silk satin that has a slight pink tint. The spread is backed in a fragile, paper-thin apricot-pink silk, and finished with a silk fringe that exactly matches the color of the embroidery.

92 in. wide by 111 in. long
Owned by the Tilghman family
Used in Maryland and Philadelphia
Made in Macao, China for the Western market
73.34 Gift of Mr. George W. King in memory of Effie Tilghman Wallis King

CORNER

BORDER

Victorian Crewelwork Bedspread

About 1850-1870

"Elegant spreads are made of satin with rich lace insertions and trimmings. Some are made of plush enriched with embroidery, and both owe their beauty to richness of texture and color."

—"BEDSPREADS," *Maine Farmer*, October 30, 1890

This rather unusual bedspread uses brilliant multicolored wool to embroider naturalistic flowers and grapes on a white cotton ground. In combining wool embroidery with a cotton ground, it recalls the wool-on-linen crewelwork of the previous century. In the succeeding hundred years, however, the style has evolved greatly. The exotic and stylized designs derived from Jacobean-era embroidery have been replaced with natural and botanically identifiable flowers, reflecting the Victorians' love of gardens and naturalism.

Floral designs are nothing new either to textiles or to bed coverings made by women, but the Victorian era surpassed all previous ones when it came to the love of garden design and botany. The 19th century saw the introduction of innumerable new species of plants, whether from importation from exotic parts of the world, or from experimentation in propagation and hybridization. Botany even became an acceptable science for women to pursue, even while the necessity and appropriateness of women's higher education were still being debated. It is in this context that we see the enormous outpouring of floral-themed quilts and counterpanes of the mid-19th century.

Square blocks on point, 15 inches square, are machine-sewn together; there are twenty squares, with fourteen triangular half blocks along the sides, and four quarter blocks in the corners. A pieced border with an embroidered vine completes the spread. The excellence of the embroidery, which is almost entirely done in satin stitch with French knots at the center of some of the flowers, is not matched by the quality of the sewing. The blocks do not always meet at their corners, and the spread does not lie flat. Horizontally, rows of larger bouquets alternate with rows of grape clusters and smaller bunches. Diagonally, rows alternate between either larger and smaller flowers, or larger flowers and grape clusters. A simple leaf-and-berry border extends in discontinuous lengths on each side of the bedspread. It frames, but does not compete with the center. Overall, thoughtful arrangement of the various motifs has created a balanced but energetic design.

74 in. wide by 87 in. long
About 1850-1870
Unknown Maker
Made in the United States
2005.46   Friends of the Museum Purchase

80 inches square
Unknown Maker
Made in Pennsylvania or Ohio
9 stitches per inch
2772   Gift of Katherine Haldeman Baldridge honoring
Mrs. Anthony Wayne Cook, NSDAR President General,
1923-1926.

Stuffed Flower Vases Quilt

About 1840

This beautiful and striking quilt has garnered much attention over the years. The Index of American Design, a WPA project in the 1930s which employed artists to sketch and paint examples of American decorative and folk arts, recorded it among its selection of American quilts. In 1941, *Woman's Day* magazine photographed it on a four-poster bed as part of an article on appliqué. The article included a design for a bedspread liberally adapting the original, with four rows of flowers between rows of the scalloped border. A more faithful copy, made by a DAR member who saw the original on display at the DAR in 1945, is in the collection of the International Quilt Study Collection at the University of Nebraska, Lincoln. And at some point, according to the donor, it won a prize at the Ohio State Fair. With all this deserved admiration, it is a pity we do not know the maker.

The field consists of nine blocks, each 19-1/2 inches square. Five colorful appliqué squares alternate with four white ones. The appliqué squares have similar, but not quite identical floral arrangements in a footed vase. Three of the white blocks are quilted in designs that mimic the appliqué blocks. The final white block has a spray of flowers. All are heavily stuffed, adding depth and definition to both colored and white blocks.

The colored flowers include a variety of blooms: red roses and rosebuds; red-and-pink peony-like blooms; and bluebell-like clusters in blue and yellow, among others. Most of the fabrics are solid colors, but the stamens are made of printed cotton. The 10-inch border's flowers echo the baskets', with a simple repeating pattern. On each side of the border, always near the middle, a pale yellow bird perches, with a bead for an eye. The border flowers meander between two rows of a spring green appliquéd, scalloped border. Parallel diagonal lines of quilting set off the basket squares and the floral border; the green border is grid-quilted. The photo is oriented for the best view of the reader, but the curved corners at the photo's top suggest that that end is the foot of the bed, so that the center basket is meant to be seen by the sleeper.

The cheery colors, simplified forms and somewhat folk-art quality of the design matched the aesthetic of the "colonial revival" style of quilting of the 1920s through 1940s. It is no wonder that it was chosen for copying both by a national magazine in 1941, and by an enthusiastic quilter in 1945. But its artistry and visual appeal are timeless.

DAR MUSEUM

Embroidered Wool Counterpane

About 1830

This is a fine example of a less well-known type of bed covering: the embroidered wool blanket. To call this a blanket, however, is somewhat misleading, as it is clearly intended to be the decorative top layer for a bed. The ground fabric is made of two panels of a very heavy twill wool in cream, heavier than the usual blanket, and giving at least as much warmth as a quilt. This wool is the backdrop for variety of lovely embroidered floral motifs. A large, floral, meandering vine creates a deep border on three sides, not unlike the whitework quilts and candlewick bedspreads of this time. The vine springs in two tendrils from a "stem" in the center of the bottom of the spread. At the top in the center are two medallions with two circles composed of heart motifs. Although hearts were a popular motif and cannot always be linked to love and marriage, the presence of the two heart-filled circles cannot help but raise speculation that this spread (though narrow) was made for use by two people.

In the center field, rows of floral sprays alternate with rows of abstract roundels in the center. These roundels are almost identical to some of the stylized flower sprigs. This motif is somewhat reminiscent of Pennsylvania Dutche motifs, although nothing is known about this spread's regional origins. Despite the stylized nature of these motifs, the flowers are overall more naturalistic than those of earlier, crewelwork-style blooms. The rows of flowers and roundels are placed somewhat irregularly, a charming indication that the maker placed motifs as she went along rather than laying everything out beforehand. A chain of circles forms a simple border to balance the elaborate vine, and a 3-inch deep blue wool fringe made of thin two-ply wool completes the spread. The design fills the space without crowding it, while the monochrome color scheme keeps the lively design from being overpowering. We can appreciate every component of the embroidery, and enjoy the total effect as well.

78 in. wide by 92 in. long
Unknown Maker
Possibly made in New England
2005.4   Friends of the Museum Purchase

"The young ladies at this Institute are to be employed four hours daily in housekeeping, the manufacture of wool, useful needlework, the culture of silk, appropriate parts of gardening, &c."
—"OBERLIN FEMALE PROFESSORSHIP ASSOCIATE OF NEW-YORK," *New York Evangelist*, April 4, 1835

DAR MUSEUM

"They were holding a somewhat noisy consultation whether the quilt should be quilted in gingerbread, shells, herring-bone, flowers, or straight work, and 'what do you say, Hannah?' was asked at least by half a dozen voices, all speaking at once.
'As it is a patch-work quilt,' she replied, 'and will not show the quality of the work like a glossy shalloon, I should, were it mine, quilt it in shells.'
'That is what I think,' said Mary, 'for I shall want to quilt my sky blue one in flowers, and I already have one done in herring-bone.'"

—"A COUNTRY COQUETTE," by Caroline Orne, *Ladies' National Magazine*, July 1845

Elizabeth Ann's SUNBURST QUILT

1840-41

At a distance, this quilt is handsome enough, with its soft blue-and-white palette and orderly rows of well-executed sunburst medallions. But a closer look reveals its maker's true artistry. Innumerable rows of close-set, parallel, diagonal stitching lines set off extraordinary stuffed-work between each medallion. Large pineapples with gracefully curving leaves, grape clusters with energetically twining stems, fat baskets filled with fruit stuffed almost to real-life three-dimensionality, and abundant cornucopias fill the larger spaces between the pieced rows. In the smaller spaces between the medallions are feathered wreaths with crossed-grid centers The stuffed work around the edge of the center field contains a series of large ivy leaves, sunflowers, half feathered wreaths with cross-grid centers, pomegranates and a large, stuffed-work-filled scallop variation. This scallop shape encloses a highly stylized vase with a barely recognizable plantlike motif emerging from it. In all, Elizabeth Ann Darst demonstrates unusual versatility and originality in her stuffed-work designs.

The border around all four sides has a 1-1/4 inch wide blue zigzag, which rather charmingly fails to turn the corners with any regularity or symmetry. The blue fabric used throughout is a tiny print consisting of rows of 1/8 inch or smaller lines or "dashes" in two shades of blue and in white; from not far away, it blends to seem like a solid pale blue. In the corners of each zig and zag are stuffed-work scallop shells. The zigzags are outline-quilted, with two additional rows of stitching inside them. The sunburst medallions have two rows of outline quilting on all the pieces, both blue and white, with a grid at the center. The medallion circles are pieced, not appliquéd. (This stunning work was done by Elizabeth Harness Bierce, the daughter of Martha Harness Darst who made the blue and white quilt on page **26**, just prior to her 1841 marriage.) Martha Harness Darst had moved from Hardy County, Virginia (now West Virginia), where she completed her quilt, immediately after her marriage in 1817 to Isaac Darst; Elizabeth, their first child, was born in Ohio in 1818. It is wonderful to have two quilts from the same family, and intriguing to see the love of stuffed work, and the blue-and-white palette, continue from one generation to the next.

104 in. wide by 107 in. long
Made by Elizabeth Ann Darst Bierce (1818-1901)
Assisted by Martha Harness Darst (1788-1854)
Circleville, Ohio
7-8 stitches per inch
2006.38   Friends of the Museum Purchase

DAR MUSEUM

69 in. wide by 59 in. long
Made by Arkansas Katherine Shely Fritzien
(1836-1903)
Jessamine County, Kentucky
2007.19   Gift of Miriam Baublitz

Arkansas Fritzien's CENTENNIAL PATCHWORK

1876

This patchwork and embroidered quilt was made by Arkansas or "Arkie" Katherine Fritzien, of Jessamine County, Kentucky. Family history relates that it was exhibited at the Philadelphia Centennial Exposition, and won a prize. It is certainly a colorful and masterly work with professional-caliber embroidery. It combines a large, pieced, central hexagon and pieced border with elaborate floral embroidery in the corners, using shaded silk embroidery floss to give each flower a more elaborate appearance, and set off against a black taffeta background.

The patchwork hexagon is formed of smaller hexagons, each with a six-pointed star made with two colors and a circle at the center. The diamond pieces which form the stars are made from solid-color taffetas on a black taffeta background, while most of the circular centers are made of striped or plaid ribbed silks. The stars are arranged in concentric rows around the black center hexagon: a row of yellow and green stars is surrounded by a yellow and blue row. The last row has yellow and blue stars in the corner and a variety of colors in between.

The patchwork areas are quilted in outline stitching. The border's red triangles between the stars, however, contain abstract foliate designs resembling fleurs-de-lis, and the corners have graceful abstract motifs. The back of the quilt is made of a mauve silk taffeta, quilted in its own design, which does not appear on the front of the quilt. A diamond grid with double rows of stitches adorns most of the back, while a series of abstract scrolls meanders around the border. A mauve taffeta-covered cording forms the binding of the quilt.

Three embroideries mark this as a centennial celebration. A pair of crossed American flags appears at center top and center bottom, each in the narrow floral borders between the outer edge and the central hexagon, with "1776" between the flags on the top and "1876" between the flags at the bottom. In the patchwork's very center, an American eagle holds a flag in his beak, and olive branches in his talons.

The quilt is much too small for a bed, but was made instead as a decorative textile for the parlor. This sort of patchwork was just coming into style about this time. Log cabin quilts and crazy quilts are the more frequently seen examples of this use of patchwork, but those are invariably unquilted. A two-sided quilt with a crazy quilt design dated 1893 on one side, uses a design almost identical to this centennial quilt (and almost identical in size, but without embroidery) on its reverse.[1] Not only does this similarity raise questions about a common design source, but the two-sided textile is edged with a silk cord with tassels at the corner, like the DAR's log cabin on page 92.

The quiltmaker's name, Arkansas, strikes us as unusual, but naming children after geographical locations was, and still is, fairly common. A search of the 1870 census finds, for example, nearly every state and territory of the U.S. represented. Popularity varies greatly, from two people named Connecticut, to 702 named Texas, to over 4100 named Tennessee—and over 9500 named America. Arkansas appears 274 times, and that excludes the many possible variations (misspellings and nicknames). Today, popular names for children include Dakota, Brittany (a region of France), and Devon (for Devonshire, an English county). As testimony to the excitement over the nation's 100th anniversary, the 1880 census reveals 108 people named Centennial, born within a year or two of 1876.

1 Robert Shaw, *American Quilts: The Democratic Art, 1780-2007* (London and New York: Sterling, 2009), 154-5.

DAR MUSEUM

"By the time our mistress arrived at home; where the first thing she did was to dispose of us in a richly embroidered Needle-case, which, along with a new thimble and scissors, was deposited in a fine work-bag."

—"THE ADVENTURES OF A NEEDLE," *The Atheneum; or Spirit of the English Magazines*, February 1, 1823.

Embroidered Calamanco Quilt

About 1820

While the wholecloth wool calamanco quilts of New England (see the example on page 18 are relatively familiar, the embroidered wool ones like this are less well known and rather rare. This example features delicate silk, crewelwork-style, floral sprigs and sprays on a chocolate-brown ground, with a darker brown wool border on the bottom and sides. There are ten variations on the flowers, with anywhere from one to six blooms in white, yellow and pink-and-red combinations. Though somewhat irregularly arranged, a basic pattern of large/small/large/small is discernable both vertically and horizontally. However, the embroiderer erred, or did not yet have her pattern figured out when she worked the upper left corner; the number and arrangement of flowers is irregular for the first few rows on the left.

On the other hand, her quilting is well-thought-out. The border corners have feather wreaths, while each side of the border has a meandering feather vine typical of New England wool quilts. In the center of the main part of the quilt is a 17-inch feather wreath, which surrounds four embroidered floral sprigs. Quilted flowers are spaced in the brown background between rows of embroidery. The background quilting is diagonal lines, divided into four quadrants, which radiate out from the central wreath to each corner of the quilt. The upper and lower quadrants' quilting goes from lower left to upper right; the side quadrants are the opposite. The darker brown border, 15-1/4 inches deep, is quilted with a large meandering feather vine of the sort found in so many calamanco quilts. Eight-petalled flowers and six-pointed stars are quilted both inside the curves of the feather vine, and between the embroideries. The quilt is backed, as so many calamanco quilts are, with plain-woven yellow wool.

Although the identity of the maker is now unknown, we are fortunate that her work has been preserved by the various hands it passed through in appreciation of her artistic expression.

86 inches square
Unknown Maker
Made in New England
7 stitches per inch
2009.50   Gift of Quilts, Inc.

"Economy of time must, one would think, have been the most necessary of economies to the old-time housewives. With so many things to do, how did they find time to make those marvels of misplaced industry, the patched bed-quilts?"

—"AN AMERICAN LADY'S OCCUPATION, SEVENTY YEARS AGO," *Lippincott's Magazine of Popular Literature and Science*, April 1875.

Biblical Stories Quilt

1874

The history of this quilt must be pieced together from small scraps of information. The worn-and-torn label "John Atkins-," the donor's memory of its being made by a great-aunt Josephine Miller, and the presence of a John and Josephine Atkinson in the 1880 census in Baltimore County, Maryland, where the rest of the donor's family lived, are among the clues that allow us to say with some confidence that this was made by Josephine Miller Atkinson. The date is supplied in the lower left corner beneath the corner basket.

The family knew this as the "Biblical Stories" quilt. While not explicitly showing a biblical scene, it contains a wealth of animals, and includes a snake in three of the four quadrants, suggesting the Garden of Eden. Josephine created a striking and original blend of piecing and appliqué, starting with the widely used four-block quilt template. Four quadrants filled with flora and fauna appliqués are defined by a large, central, eight-pointed star, with smaller eight-pointed stars near it in each quadrant. The quadrants are divided by what first appears to be a sort of narrow sashing or border, varying in color from brown to blue to pale yellow; but on closer inspection, these are seen to be trees or branches with multicolored leaves diverging from each one. In each quadrant, Josephine randomly arranged similar animals and plants without regard to scale or logic, quirkily filling up each field with a profusion of motifs until no more could fit, but anchored by a floral basket in each corner.

An oversized wooden button, covered in orange cotton, rather curiously punctuates the very center of the center star. (This is so large and unwieldy that it is difficult to imagine sleeping under it.) A strong, solid-green, scallop-edged border surrounds the scenes, and a brown binding is the final edging for the quilt.

The date of 1874, appliquéd below one corner basket, puts the quilt in the context of its day. There was a spate of biblical-themed quilts made in the third quarter of the 19th century, seemingly in response to the contemporary debates surrounding Charles Darwin's research, published first in *The Origin of Species* in 1859 and later in *The Descent of Man* in 1871, followed swiftly by *The Expression of the Emotion in Man and Animal*; the latter two explore his earlier theory in more detail. "Garden of Eden" quilts, and others with biblical themes, were thus being made at a time when the new and shocking concept of evolution was being hotly debated in American culture.

The baskets and the animals are strongly reminiscent of Baltimore album quilts, which were popular just a generation before this quilt was made, testifying to the lasting popularity and influence of those quilts. The quilt's design shows Josephine to have been a product of her time, yet wonderfully individualistic as a designer.

88 in. wide by 81 in. long
Made by Josephine Miller Atkinson (b. c.1836)
Baltimore County, Maryland
97.12   Gift of Verna Helen Bitzer Walter in honor of Josephine Miller Atkinson

Be still— and know that I am God.

Teaching them to observe all things whatsoever I have commanded you: and lo I am with you alway even unto the end of the world amen

If we say we have no sin, we deceive ourselves and the truth is not in us.

If we say that we have not sinned we make him a liar, and his word is not in us Casting all your care upon him for he careth for you

Take my yoke upon you and learn of me; for I am meek and lowly in heart: and ye shall find rest unto your souls. For my yoke is easy, and my burden is light.

He that believeth on the son hath everlasting life and shall not come into condemnation but is passed from death unto life

All we like sheep have gone astray we have turned every one to his own way and the Lord hath laid on him the iniquity of us all.

but i say unto you which hear love your enemies do good to them which hate you bless them that curse you and pray for them which despitefully use you

So christ was once offered to bear the sins of many and unto them that look for him shall he appear the second time without sin unto salvation

Come unto me all ye that labor and are heavy laden and I will give you rest

And this is the record, that God hath given to us eternal life, and this life is in his son. We love him because he first loved us

And Jesus said unto them I am the bread of life he that cometh to me shall never hunger and he that believeth on me shall never thirst

God, be merciful to me a sinner They that be whole need not a physician but they that are sick all have sinned and come short of the glory of god

Let no man say when he is tempted, I am tempted of god for god cannot be tempted with evil, neither tempteth he any man: He that loveth not, knoweth not god; for God is love.

Behold what manner of love the Father hath bestowed upon us that we should be called the sons of God therefore the world knoweth us not because it knew him not

There is none righteous, no not one; and except a man be born again, he cannot see the kingdom of god.

"Instead of making articles for sale, let them employ themselves in altering cast-off garments for Sunday school children. In putting their old gowns together and quilting warm coverlets for the sick and the destitute. Those who have fine old linen or should they prefer it they might make up linen for poor Students of Theology. I would also suggest a plan for furnishing a fund for Missionary or Bible purposes."

—"Remarks on the Proposed Plan of Female Circles of Industry: To the Editor of the Christian Herald, Dorcus" *The Christian Herald and Seaman's Magazine*, May 18, 1822.

Redwork Scripture Bedspread

About 1860

This unusual Bible verse spread used Turkey red embroidery thread as its only method of decoration, decades before the more famous heyday of "redwork" embroidered bedspreads. "Turkey red" was not an actual dye substance, but a newly developed, multi-step dye process, which produced a bright and singularly colorfast red.

Mary McDowell used the red thread to create a red and white embroidered bedspread almost entirely embellished with Biblical inscriptions. Sixteen linen blocks, approximately 16 inches square, are pieced with 1-inch plain linen sashing. The spread is backed with a single panel of cotton and has no filling or quilting. The blocks are embroidered in red cotton thread with verses from the King James Version of the Bible; several squares combine more than one verse. Ten inscriptions are from the Gospels; eleven are from the Epistles; and two are from the Old Testament (Psalms and Isaiah). The upper left block is decorated with birds and flowers, which adds emphasis to its verse, "Be still, and know that I am God" (Psalm 46:10). In a way, this serves as an introduction to the quilt, inviting the viewer to pause, read the verses, and rest under them. It makes perfect sense that the verses include restful and comforting ones such as "Come unto me, all ye that labour and are heavy laden, and I will give you rest" (Matthew 28:20, second column, third row).

The corner blocks' inscriptions are embroidered at an angle. When viewers observe the entire bedspread head-on, this change of angle causes the remainder of the blocks to form the shape of a cross, a clever and subtle effect on the part of the maker.

This counterpane was said by the donor, Mary's granddaughter, to have been exhibited at the Centennial Exposition in 1876 in Philadelphia. There was a large exhibit of fine needlework shown there, but precise records of objects and their lenders are elusive, so we cannot confirm this story. Whatever the case, Mary made a striking quilt that proclaimed her faith and invited the visitor to take from it physical and spiritual rest as well as aesthetic pleasure.

75 in. wide by 75.5 in. long
Made by Mary McDowell (b. 1819)
Probably made in Philadelphia, Pennsylvania
Machine-pieced and hand embroidered
5 stitches per inch
77.32 Gift of Mildred Burns

Eagle Bedspread
About 1864
76 in. wide by 88 in. long
Made by Margaret English Dodge (c. 1781-1873)
Painted by John Wood Dodge (1807-1893)
Brooklyn, New York
88.23 Gift of Margaret Todd

Civil War Flag Bedspreads

Margaret English Dodge of Brooklyn, New York wore her Union colors proudly, making at least three known bedspreads or textiles based on the American flag during the Civil War. One was a silk twin of our eagle bedspread, and was displayed at the famous Brooklyn Sanitary Fair of 1864, which raised money for the Union troops. The Brooklyn Eagle newspaper made mention of "a unique and handsome bed spread, in the form of the National banner, the workmanship of Mrs. Margaret E. Dodge, aged 80 years. The painting in the centre of it is by Dodge the well known miniature painter. It attracts deserved attention." It also earned Mrs. Dodge a "diploma" (award) for "a very meritorious bed-quilt."

The miniatures painter, artist of the appliquéd eagle, was Margaret's son, John Wood Dodge. Dodge had begun his career as a sign painter, which undoubtedly influenced his eagle. J.W. Dodge had been living in Tennessee when the Civil War broke out, and had to move his Northern family hurriedly back to New York for the duration of the war. While there, he lent his skills to two of his mother's bedspreads: the silk one shown at the Brooklyn Fair, and the DAR's, which is made of cotton.

The silk one was subsequently presented to President Lincoln by the secretary of the fair, Rev. Frederick A. Farley, who described it as "a silk 'Bed-Spread,' formed of the National Colors, and emblazoned with the Stars and Stripes and the national Eagle. …this fine specimen of needle-work is from the hands of…Mrs. Margaret E. Dodge, [aged] eighty-one years; while the painting is the work of her equally loyal son, J.W. Dodge, a Union Refugee from Tennessee." (Perhaps, given the letter's further pointed references to the family's land lost in Tennessee, the spread was sent in hopes that the President would somehow assist in the land's recovery.) In any case, Lincoln wrote a thank-you letter offering "my most cordial thanks for the beautiful present transmitted by you." This spread's current whereabouts are unknown.

The DAR's cotton version of the eagle bedspread may be an exact, or is at least a close copy of the silk one as described. It is a combination of piecing and appliqué, the stripes being pieced while the stars are appliquéd. The eagle is also appliquéd, as is the shield on its chest. The spread is backed in cotton and bound with a machine-sewn woven tape.

Peterson's Magazine Flag Bedspred
1861-1863
66 in. wide by 78 in. long
Made by Margaret English Dodge (c. 1781-1873)
Brooklyn, New York
87.67.1 Gift of Elsa Sutton Dorrance in memory of
Nellie T. Sutton and George Alfred Sutton

The second Dodge bedspread is made according to a pattern that appeared in *Peterson's Magazine* in July 1861, shortly after the war broke out. *Peterson's* and its rival fashion magazine, *Godey's*, later tried to largely ignore the war that divided its readers, so as not to offend and lose half of them; but clearly this policy was not yet in place when this issue went to press. The center field, and border, both have thirty-four stars, the number of states in the Union from 1861 (when Kansas was admitted) until 1863 (when West Virginia split off from Virginia and was accepted into the Union as a new state, the thirty-fifth). A quilted version of this bedspread design is in the Smithsonian collection.

Neither of these spreads shows much finesse in the actual needlework. Perhaps Margaret's fine needlework days were behind her: she was, after all, over eighty. They are simply pieced and unquilted. The eagle's being painted rather than appliquéd may also reflect a desire to minimize the sewing required, but Margaret may equally have been making the most of her son's fame and skill to make the textile more worthy of notice.

The two bedspreads were handed down in the Dodge family and were donated by two sisters. Such patriotic-themed quilts and bedspreads were often made and sold to raise money for the troops at United States Sanitary Commission fairs and other events, but as these were passed down in the family, they clearly were not intended as such. However, we have the evidence of Mrs. Dodge's making at least one bedspread for the Brooklyn fair, and she may have made others for that or other fundraisers.

"We had a patriotic quilting party a few weeks since, in the open air under the shade of some maples from whose pendant boughs the stars and stripes gaily fluttered in the breeze, while beneath were twenty quilts in process of completions by the loyal women of our city, young, middle-aged and aged."

—"CORRESPONDENCE, BY C.C. MASON" *Zion's Herald and Wesleyan Journal*, September 21, 1864

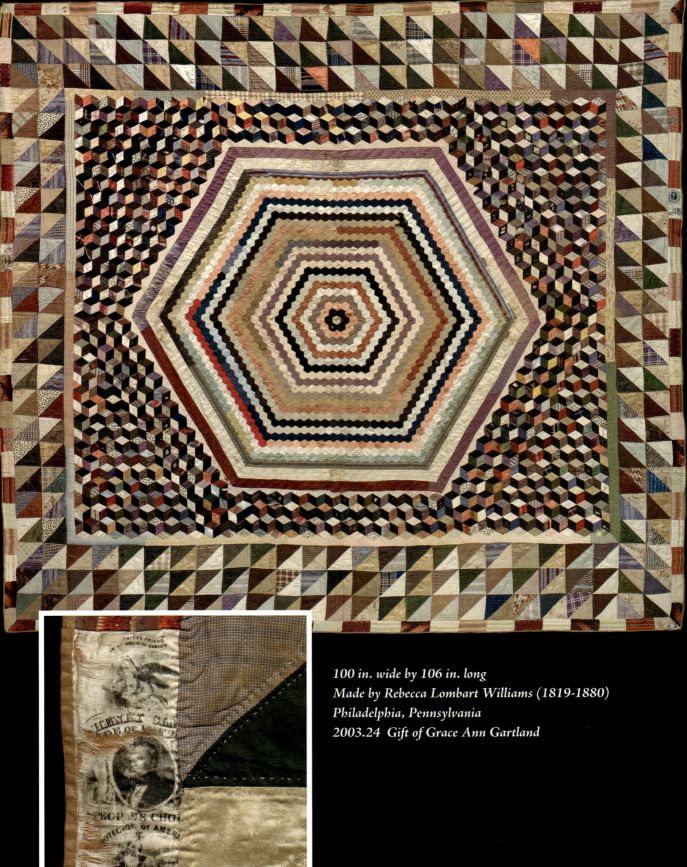

100 in. wide by 106 in. long
Made by Rebecca Lombart Williams (1819-1880)
Philadelphia, Pennsylvania
2003.24 Gift of Grace Ann Gartland

DAR MUSEUM

Henry Clay Campaign
Silk Counterpane

About 1844

Despite having been made three-quarters of a century before women could vote, this silk counterpane gives hints of its maker's political convictions. Two silk ribbons from the 1844 U.S. presidential campaign are discreetly placed among the outer edge's rectangular pieced border. A third promotes "Abstinence."

The center of the design is a large hexagon comprised of concentric circles of small hexagons in a field of diamonds in a "Tumbling Blocks" configuration. The orientation of the blocks varies. An outer border is composed of squares bisected into light and dark triangles. The fabrics include prints, satins, brocades, plaids and plain weave silks. The central hexagon is composed of simple concentric rows. The three rows of tumbling blocks surround the hexagon, each side oriented toward the center. In the corners, beyond those first three rows, the blocks all face the same way, except in the upper left corner. An outer border of three rows of triangles is outlined finally by a single row of brick-shaped pieces. The top is not quilted, but only backed in glazed cotton and finished with a bias silk binding.

The most remarkable feature of this handsome bedspread is the inclusion of three printed silk ribbons, two from the Henry Clay presidential campaign of 1844. One says "Henry Clay/The Pride of America" and the other, "The People's Choice/Protector of America." The third ribbon contains only one legible word, "Abstinence." Henry Clay, a Whig, ran against James K. Polk, a Democrat, for president in 1844. Clay opposed annexation of Texas, at the time an independent republic. President Tyler presented a treaty for annexation to the U.S Senate in April 1844. Clay, who believed annexation might lead to war with Mexico, reached out to women, who, although lacking the vote, might influence the men of their family. The Clay campaign hoped that women would wish to support the party that was trying to avoid a war to which their husbands and sons might be sent. In the end, Clay lost out to the country's expansionist mood.

It is interesting to find Clay campaign ribbons on a bed covering from Philadelphia, the center of the abolitionist movement, because Clay had publicly denounced the antislavery movement. However, politics of the time were complicated—as politics always are—and it may be that the anti-annexation plank of Clay's platform was enough to win Rebecca Williams's support. The third ribbon proclaiming abstinence suggests that Rebecca, like other men and women of her time, supported the temperance movement. Along with abolition, temperance was one of the first political issues to inspire women to unite in organizations and work for social change. Unlike the later temperance movement, the goal at this time was to use moral suasion to encourage individuals to change their habits, rather than working for legal prohibitions. Even so, women's involvement in social issues of the day sparked a good deal of criticism. Victorian women were supposed to stay in their proper, divinely ordained, domestic sphere and not become involved in public matters. However, the evils of excessive drinking by a father or husband had obvious harmful effects on the family, including the possible loss of income and employment that a family relied upon. Thus, temperance was an issue that many women judged to be directly linked to their role as protector and moral leader of the household.

We cannot know to what extent Rebecca Williams supported these political and social causes, but she gave us clues to her convictions in the piecing of her counterpane. Altogether, this domestic textile is testimony to its maker's interests beyond the boundaries of her home and in the wider world.

"Fifty thousand pocket handkerchiefs for boys and girls, were printed in Philadelphia county in one single day, in the last spring, by rollers moved by water, covered with copper and engraved with figures and flowers. These rollers can be engraved with any figure or pattern, and will print with one color upon a white or blue, buff or other dyed ground."

—"Great Britain Destroying her own manufactures and promoting our manufactures," *Weekly Register*, July 18, 1812

George Washington Commemorative Counterpane

About 1785-1800

Many printed textiles celebrating American independence and its heroes were produced in France, England and Scotland beginning at the end of the Revolution in 1783, and continued in popularity for some years. It should not surprise us that English manufacturers were willing to portray subjects favorable to the Americans; not only were they businessmen willing to capitalize on a new market, but many liberal Englishmen had been more or less sympathetic to the Americans' cause.

The allegorical scenes represented on this fabric are grandiloquently titled "America Presenting at the Altar of Liberty, Medallions of Her Illustrious Sons." The Illustrious Sons in this case include military and political heroes of American independence, from John Jay to less well-remembered figures such as Baron von Steuben, shown in double profile portraits in a large medallion. One medallion is held by the figure of Peace, who symbolically tramples on a shield with the English flag's Union cross on it. Washington appears in person, being crowned with a laurel wreath by Fame while Minerva (Roman goddess of both war and wisdom) presents more medallions at Liberty's Altar. Liberty, identifiable by her Liberty Pole crowned with its floppy Liberty cap, sits atop her altar. The counterpane is bound with a strip of red and white printed tape.

Allegorical paintings glorifying military heroes or monarchs were an art historical tradition of 17th and 18th century Europe. Goddesses and allegorical figures such as those seen here were depicted in pamphlets as well as ceramics, furnishings and textiles, and would have been recognized by much of the American public; they were, in their time, on par with our figures of Uncle Sam and the political parties' donkey and elephant symbols.

This design has survived in several versions, in red, black, purple and other colors typical of these toiles. Engraved copper plates were used to create these prints, which allowed finer detail than the standard wood block printing techniques. The figure of Washington is based on an engraving of John Trumbull's portrait. Several of the portraits in the medallions are from drawings by Pierre-Eugène Du Simitière for his series entitled "Eminent Americans," engraved in Paris by Benoit Louis Prevost. Two pirated sets of this series were engraved in London in 1783. These pirated sets could have been used by the English manufacturer of the copper plates used in this design as a basis for the other patriots' portraits.

The donor traced this counterpane through her maternal line, but there are too many female ancestors at the time this counterpane must have been made, to hazard a guess at its maker. Some branches of the family lived near Albany, New York as early as 1780; other branches were in Fairfield County, Connecticut and Berkshire County, Massachusetts. We cannot say more than that it was almost certainly made in one of those states. Whoever owned it was showing her pride in her new country, wherever she was.

91 in. wide by 97 in. long
Unknown Maker
Made in New York, Connecticut or Massachusetts
62.28 *Gift of Margaret Luther*

"Every thing here was the best and neatest kind. A suit of curtains hung round the bed, the counterpane was white as snow, and the bed-linen was fresh and fragrant."

—"THE PHILADELPHIA DUN," *The Illinois Monthly Magazine*, November 1830

Mercy Deuel's WHITEWORK COUNTERPANE

1828

Mercy Deuel's counterpane contains many design features typical of bedspreads and quilts of its time, but its most remarkable feature is undoubtedly the large medallion near the top with large letters proclaiming it to be "PROPERTY/ of/ Mercy E. Deuel/of/Cambridge/1828." Names, dates and even names of hometowns are often inscribed on quilts and especially on whitework counterpanes; but the large, capitalized "PROPERTY" is distinctive.

Recent research into Mercy's life has revealed that she never married, but lived all her life with various relatives in Cambridge, New York, north of Albany near the Vermont border. In the 1850 census, she is living with a niece, and by the 1870 census, she is living with a different nephew. It is understandable that, never having her own home or, probably, furnishings—perhaps not always having even a room or space of her own—she might have wanted to lay undisputed claim to bed linens of her own making. Household textiles have traditionally been considered the property of the women of the household, even when women had no legal property rights to speak of, so Mercy was building on tradition by inscribing her name on her handiwork. But she was also asserting her rights to something of her own in households where she was never mistress.

Mercy used a variation on the framed medallion layout for her counterpane. The ground fabric is a cotton in a diaper-weave, or diamond-shaped overshot. The sides are selvedges and the top and bottom are seamed. The counterpane's layout has a wide border on all sides, taking up about a third of the width on each side, leaving a narrow central area for a center medallion. This central area is split among a top border; the inscription, which is contained within a stylized, simplified, swag border; and a small Tree of Life design. The Tree of Life is rather spindly, and sprouts from a large vase, with birds flanking the "trunk." The border is a vigorous, meandering, leafy vine, whose tendrils emerge from two vases at the lower corners. Tulips, Tudor Roses, and enormous strawberries bloom on the vine, making it, too, a sort of Tree of Life motif. All this is accomplished with a flat backstitch using a heavy, two-ply cotton, roving thread. Mercy had good reason, beyond identifying her property, to proudly display her name on her counterpane, for it is a beautiful textile.

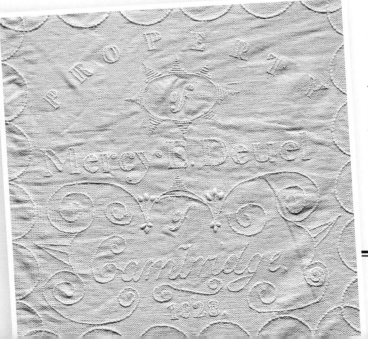

80 in. wide by 88 in. long
Made by Mercy E. Deuel (1796-1872)
Cambridge, Washington County, New York
62.181 Gift of Violet R. Ford

"To raise the virtues animate the bliss

And sweeten all the toils of human life:

This be the female dignity and praise.

It has frequently happened that chance has afforded me the opportunity of observing the actions of females, when assembled in considerable numbers at a ball, tea-party, or quilting, and frequently have been delighted and highly entertained with their conviviality and sociability;"

—"FOR THE VISITOR THE OBSERVER,"
Ladies' Visitor, April 18, 1820

DAR MUSEUM

EMBROIDERIES

The embroidery designs shown are a sampling of the many patterns featured on the antique quilts. These may be enlarged for hand embroidery or are available for machine embroidery (all formats) on CD-ROM from Martha Pullen Company.

Arkansas Fritzien's
Centennial Patchwork

Arkansas Fritzien's
Centennial Patchwork

Arkansas Fritzien's
Centennial Patchwork

Arkansas Fritzien's
Centennial Patchwork

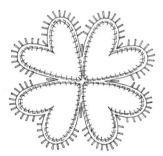

Julia Hosford's
Crazy Quilt

Julia Hosford's
Crazy Quilt

Julia Hosford's
Crazy Quilt

Arkansas Fritzien's
Centennial Patchwork

Arkansas Fritzien's
Centennial Patchwork

Victorian Crewelwork
Bedspread

Embroidered
Calamanco Quilt

Victorian Crewelwork
Bedspread

Embroidered Calamanco Quilt

Embroidered Calamanco Quilt

Embroidered Calamanco Quilt

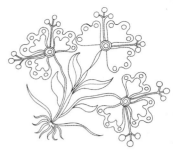
Embroidered Calamanco Quilt

Victorian Crewelwork Bedspread

Victorian Crewelwork Bedspread

Anna Hall's Crazy Quilt

Victorian Crewelwork Bedspread

Arkansas Fritzien's Centennial Patchwork

Arkansas Fritzien's Centennial Patchwork

Arkansas Fritzien's Centennial Patchwork

Arkansas Fritzien's Centennial Patchwork

Arkansas Fritzien's Centennial Patchwork

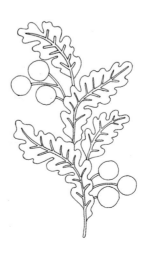
Victorian Crewelwork Bedspread

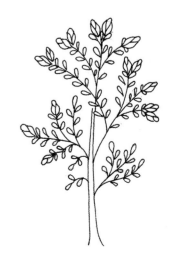
Julia Hosford's Crazy Quilt